University
of Michigan
Business
School Management Series

INNOVATIVE SOLUTIONS TO THE
PRESSING PROBLEMS OF BUSINESS

The mission of the University of Michigan Business School Management Series is to provide accessible, practical, and cutting-edge solutions to the most critical challenges facing businesspeople today. The UMBS Management Series provides concepts and tools for people who seek to make a significant difference in their organizations. Drawing on the research and experience of faculty at the University of Michigan Business School, the books are written to stretch thinking while providing practical, focused, and innovative solutions to the pressing problems of business.

Also available in the UMBS series:

For additional information on any of these titles or future
titles in the series, visit www.umbsbooks.com.

Executive Summary

Some companies repeatedly dazzle us with outstanding decisions. We marvel: "Another stroke of genius! How do they *do* that, time after time?" By contrast, other companies have a knack for deciding badly. Again we marvel: "Wow, they shot themselves in the foot again! What were they thinking—*this* time?" What best explains the difference between companies that decide well and those that do not? Do people in the former companies understand their businesses better? Do they use better formulas? Are they just plain *smarter?* Or is it all simply a matter of luck?

None of the above. The real key is "decision management," a little-recognized but crucial element of every manager's portfolio of core responsibilities. Decision management consists of the myriad actions that a company's managers take—wittingly and, more often, unwittingly—that affect how the people surrounding them go about their decision work. To the extent that the resulting decisions are sound ones, the company flourishes. But to the degree that they are not, the company struggles and may even run a serious risk of collapse.

Actually, decision management has even greater significance, far more than most of us realize. For reasons decision scientists now understand, the average executive seldom attributes a company's troubles or triumphs to its decision making and, in turn, its decision management. But if, for instance, a company is stumbling badly in the marketplace, it is entirely legitimate (and motivating) to ask: "Why didn't they make decisions that would have precluded these calamities?" The answer is that the company's leaders are managing its decisions poorly, in large measure because they rarely even *think* about how the company decides.

This book is a manual for creating and sustaining stellar decision management practices, ones that foster decisions that can keep your company among the leaders in its industry. The book starts with a discussion of what the art of decision management entails (Chapter One). The core of the conceptual analysis that guides the book's prescriptions is this key insight: Virtually every practical decision problem demands the resolution of ten fundamental or *cardinal* decision issues. These issues range from judging whether a decision is actually called for at all to ensuring that a preferred course of action will be implemented. When a company makes a superb decision, this means that the company's deciders have done a superb job of resolving every one of the cardinal decision issues as it materialized in the decision problem at hand. Conversely, a failed decision signals that the deciders fell short—perhaps catastrophically short—in how they addressed at least one of those issues. Quite simply, a good decision manager is a manager who does whatever works in order to make sure that deciders resolve every cardinal issue effectively for every decision problem facing the company.

After an introduction of essential concepts and tools (Chapter Two), the chapters that constitute the heart of the book (Chapters Three through Eight) address the ten cardinal decision issues. Each issue is illustrated vividly and concretely in terms of real-life situations that every manager can appreciate. These situations are then analyzed in terms of fundamental principles and specific decision management techniques that managers can use to craft creative ways of ensuring that deciders in their companies handle such situations with consummate skill.

All change efforts, from personal self-improvement programs to initiatives intended to transform a corporate culture, have a history of dying quiet but sure deaths from neglect. The book therefore closes (Chapter Nine) with a discussion of why this happens and what specific things you can do to greatly reduce the odds that your (and your company's) efforts to sustain stellar decision management practices will suffer the same fate.

Decision Management

How to Assure Better Decisions in Your Company

J. Frank Yates

JOSSEY-BASS
A Wiley Imprint
www.josseybass.com

Published by Jossey-Bass
A Wiley Imprint
989 Market Street, San Francisco, CA 94103-1741   www.josseybass.com

Jossey-Bass books and products are available through most bookstores. To contact Jossey-Bass directly, call our Customer Care Department within the U.S. at (800) 956-7739, outside the U.S. at (317) 572-3993, or fax (317) 572-4002.

Jossey-Bass also publishes its books in a variety of electronic formats. Some content that appears in print may not be available in electronic books.

Library of Congress Cataloging-in-Publication Data
Yates, J. Frank (Jacques Frank), date.
   Decision management: how to assure better decisions in your company /
J. Frank Yates.—1st ed.
        p. cm.—(University of Michigan Business School management series)
   Includes bibliographical references and index.
      ISBN 0-7879-5626-0 (alk. paper)
   1. Decision making. I. Title. II. Series.
   HD30.23 .Y386 2003
   658.4'03—dc21

                                                          2002013974

FIRST EDITION
HB Printing   10 9 8 7 6 5 4 3 2 1

Contents

For Hali, Zack, Court, and
the memory of my parents
and my brother Andrew

Series Foreword

Welcome to the University of Michigan Business School Management Series. The books in this series address the most urgent problems facing business today. The series is part of a larger initiative at the University of Michigan Business School (UMBS) that ties together a range of efforts to create and share knowledge through conferences, survey research, interactive and distance training, print publications, and news media.

It is just this type of broad-based initiative that sparked my love affair with UMBS in 1984. From the day I arrived I was enamored with the quality of the research, the quality of the MBA program, and the quality of the Executive Education Center. Here was a business school committed to new lines of research, new ways of teaching, and the practical application of ideas. It was a place where innovative thinking could result in tangible outcomes.

The UMBS Management Series is one very important outcome, and it has an interesting history. It turns out that every year five thousand participants in our executive program fill out a marketing survey in which they write statements indicating the most important problems they face. One day Lucy Chin, one of our administrators, handed me a document containing all these statements. A content analysis of the data resulted in a list of forty-five pressing problems. The topics ranged from growing a company to managing personal stress. The list covered a wide territory, and I started to see its potential. People in organizations tend to be driven by a very traditional set of problems, but the solutions evolve. I went to my friends at Jossey-Bass to discuss a publishing project. The discussion eventually grew into the University of Michigan Business School Management Series— Innovative Solutions to the Pressing Problems of Business.

The books are independent of each other, but collectively they create a comprehensive set of management tools that cut across all the functional areas of business—from strategy to human resources to finance, accounting, and operations. They draw on the interdisciplinary research of the Michigan faculty. Yet each book is written so a serious manager can read it quickly and act immediately. I think you will find that they are books that will make a significant difference to you and your organization.

Robert E. Quinn, Consulting Editor
M.E. Tracy Distinguished Professor
University of Michigan Business School

Preface

From the time I began working on this book, family, friends, and colleagues have asked me the following sorts of questions over and over: "Why do you feel compelled to write that book?" "What, exactly, do you hope the book accomplishes?" "Why is that so important?" "If it's *really* that important, why hasn't it been done before?" "Why *you?*" So let me tell you, too, because as a prospective reader, you might find the answers of interest as well.

I am deeply moved by events that create radical changes in people's welfare. Good fortune excites great joy. But it is *mis*fortune that really grabs me. It stirs questions that do not easily go away: Why did that happen? Did it *have* to happen? What could have been done to keep it from happening? Is there anything *I* can do to keep it from happening again? If so, what? And that is where business and this book enter the picture.

Increasingly, our society turns to business to serve seemingly every purpose imaginable. This means that, more and more, when people experience great fortune—good or bad—it is because of what happens in some company. There are, of course, effects on company owners, as their investments multiply or evaporate according to the company's performance in the marketplace. And the owners' fortunes typically go hand in hand with those of the company's workers, their families, and their communities. At any moment and completely outside their control, these people may find themselves prospering or plunged into destitution. There are also those who are served—or not—by the company's products. Those products might meet the public's real needs or they might neglect them. Even worse, those products or the company's activities might actually do the public serious, even lethal, harm. In short, if one wants to have significant impact on what happens in people's lives, a good place to start is with the actions of companies.

What determines what happens in and to a company? Many things, of course, including the activities of competitors, market forces, weather, and what we often call chance. But even when we can point to factors outside the company, we can almost always point to the actions taken—or not taken—by people in the company itself, too. For instance, if a competitor's new product draws away customers, it is reasonable to ask why the company's people didn't make an even more attractive product that would have retained those customers. Questions like this in turn can have numerous answers, including "They had no idea what the competition was up to" or "They couldn't figure out how to make a better product" or "They didn't have the resources."

Yet, when we pursue matters further, we come to realize that underneath specific explanations like these there is a fundamental constant: decisions. The company might never have even tried to introduce an improved product because it never occurred to anybody in the company to suggest, "We need to make some decisions about updating this product." And even if the decision problem did come up, the people making the decision might have chosen to market the *wrong* new product among those considered, one that consumers find less attractive than others on the table. Or the people in decision-making positions somehow might have failed to make choices that put more creative people on product development projects or brought in the capital required to see those projects through.

Why might the people in one company generally decide better than those in another? At the most immediate level, the obvious answer is that the people in the company where more effective decisions are the norm, for some reason, decide with the aid of better resources, better tools, and better procedures. Is "some reason" simply luck, and therefore outside the reach of things that company leaders can do anything about? Quite the opposite. A company's managers, starting with the top leadership, have greater impact than anybody else on everything that happens in a company, including how the company's people decide. Although surprisingly few managers realize this, specific actions they take—or fail to take—largely dictate how and how well the people surrounding them decide among the courses open to them. These actions constitute what I call *decision management*.

When things go especially well or badly in a company, managers only rarely cite decision making as an explanation, saying, for instance, "We made a series of bad choices." And they virtually *never* appeal to what amounts to decision management, say by admitting, "We haven't trained our people to make those decisions very well." One consequence is that little or no attention and resources are devoted to improving company decision making. If a company just happens to enjoy the fruits of good decision management or suffer the consequences of weak decision management, this has occurred largely by accident rather than design, and we should expect nothing different in the future.

Why do managers neglect decision making and decision management and thereby pass over the opportunity to give their companies a distinct, bankable advantage? For numerous reasons—which incidentally represent critical challenges that any good decision manager must confront directly. One big reason for neglect is that when significant events happen in a company, everyone is naturally preoccupied with understanding and dealing with the specifics of that particular case. No one has the time or incentive to step up to higher levels and ask the key questions: "What earlier decisions did we make that put us in this fix?" or "What is it about how we function that leads us to make awful decisions like those?"

Consider the issue that managers in surveys conducted by the Michigan Business School's Executive Education Center consistently nominate as the problem they worry about most: "attracting, developing, and keeping good people." It is easy to picture the prototypical jarring event that maintains this issue on center stage: a key high-level performer decides to leave the company. ("Sorry, but I just have to get out of here," she declares.) This puts the company in a terrible bind, for she was central to critical functions in the company. She simply must be replaced, and in a hurry. So all attention is devoted to that mission, and a quick (and probably less than fully satisfactory) replacement is found. After the affair is done, the company's managers move on to the next crisis. No one gets around to examining the conditions—as well as prior decisions—that led to the loss of a vital employee, and certainly no one makes decisions to correct those conditions. With good decision management, that examination and those decisions would indeed be made—routinely. This book points toward means for creating and sustaining that kind of decision management throughout a company.

The book relies most heavily on findings in *decision science*—the body of scholarship concerned with understanding how people decide naturally and with devising means for improving on those natural inclinations. Decision science is eclectic. It draws on a host of traditional disciplines, including my parent field of psychology as well as others such as economics, statistics, sociology, mathematics, and philosophy. Within business scholarship, decision scientists find their place almost everywhere, from marketing to organizational behavior, accounting, finance, operations, and strategy. The foundations of the ideas in the book, however, extend considerably beyond decision science per se. I have called upon useful insights from a number of fields but especially upon the practical experiences of countless real managers and other decision makers I have known, studied, and taught over many years of decision scholarship. These experiences are reflected, albeit in fictionalized form, in the many examples you will find throughout the chapters (the details of which have been altered to disguise the identities of individuals and their companies).

This book integrates this knowledge and distills from it practical wisdom for better decision management in the form of proven principles, guidelines, and techniques that managers can apply every day. It will have succeeded to the degree that it inspires and helps leaders manage their companies' decisions more effectively than they do right now. For I can then rest assured that the lives of the people affected by that company—including the leaders themselves—will be demonstrably improved. In at least some small measure, the world will be a better place.

Many people made substantial contributions to this book. My greatest intellectual debts are owed to my mentors and peers in the international decision scholarship community. The intellectual debts to my colleagues in the University of Michigan's Decision Consortium and in our Judgment and Decision Laboratory are particularly significant. Yet the ideas as well as the specific cases described in the book were by far most heavily influenced by the discussions I have had with my decision management students. I am especially indebted to Jessica Brinkman, Martha Fuerstenau, Paul Grekowicz, Mark Hancock, Jennifer Holliday-Buchanan, Mark Howrey, David Ibrahim, Michael Navarro, Christina Parsons, Daniel Pompi, Sada Sankar, Scott Spencer, Jeffrey Tubbs, and Michael Zoretic.

This book would never have been written without the inspiration of Howard Kuenreuther, Pat Gurin, and George Siedel, the unflagging encouragement of Bob Quinn and Kathe Sweeney, and the generous support and resources of the Michigan Business School. Foremost among these resources are many deeply insightful faculty colleagues and our marvelous library, technical, and support staff, particularly Ollie Thomas. The character and quality of the contents have benefited immensely from the comments and reflections of many people, but especially John Carroll, Hannah Chua, Shawn Curley, Paul Estin, Xiaolan Fu, John Godek, Rich Gonzalez, Lee Green, Ju-Whei Lee, Takashi Oka, Andrea Patalano, Paul Price, Jason Riis, Hun-Tong Tan, Michael Tschirhart, Beth Veinott, and George Wright. Far and away, though, the one person most responsible for any clarity of thought and expression that might be evident in the book is John Bergez; I cannot imagine a better editorial critic and adviser anywhere. My heartfelt thanks to all.

January 2003   J. Frank Yates
Ann Arbor, Michigan

Decision Management

The Art of Decision Management

Consider this business story:

Borders is the second largest bookstore company in the United States, trailing only Barnes & Noble. In the first quarter of a recent year, the price of Borders stock plummeted more than 30 percent. Moreover, the company's slim profits during that period, from more than a thousand Borders and Waldenbooks stores, were essentially wiped away by a one-time charge of $4 million.[1]

S ituations like this are a manager's nightmare. If managers wish to avoid the kinds of disasters suffered by Borders, it is essential that they understand how and why they occur.

Suppose I ask you to speculate about what might have been the significant contributors to the troubles Borders experienced in this instance. (Give it a whirl.) If you are like most managers, you will readily bring to mind a host of plausible possibilities, including things like trends in the economy and actions taken by major competitors. What is striking and significant about the lists of potential explanations that immediately pop into managers' heads is what is typically *missing* from them—decisions. Rarely do most of us spontaneously attribute our own or others' fortunes—good or ill—to decisions. Yet when we step back and think about it, it is obvious that a company's current situation can be explained in significant measure by the adequacy of prior decisions made by the people in that company. This is so even when external forces affect a company's fate. Suppose, for example, that we could trace the dire straits Borders fell into directly to its competitors' actions. It would still be eminently reasonable to ask: "Well, why didn't Borders managers make better decisions to meet the challenge?" Yet too often such questions are never asked.

As it happens, the Borders case features a transparent connection between the company's circumstances and a prior decision. The preceding November, Borders hired Phil Pfeffer as its CEO. Shortly after his appointment, things rapidly headed south for Borders. Pfeffer was gone in April, taking with him a $4 million severance package that consumed the company's first-quarter profits (hence the one-time charge). There is no reason to think that Pfeffer's performance was the sole reason for the troubles. But at a time when Borders needed strong leadership, the Pfeffer appointment clearly failed to provide it. More important for the purposes of this discussion, there was broad consensus that the decision to hire Phil Pfeffer had been a mistake.

Even when, as in this case, we recognize the importance of decisions, we are still liable to overlook another fundamental point. Business decisions—good or bad—do not materialize out of thin air. Before someone—whether an individual or a group—makes a decision, an enormous amount of activity has occurred, which has, in effect, dictated what that decision will be. Decisions are the last link in a long chain of actions, from identifying a need to decide in the first place ("We must find a new CEO"), to marshalling the resources for deciding ("Here's how we will go about looking for candidates"), to assessing alternatives ("What does Phil bring to the table that Terry doesn't?"), to anticipating implementation issues ("If we choose Phil over Terry, what problems are we likely to run into?"). In general, decisions are only as good as the processes that produce them. It follows that, if we want to have good decisions, *we need to do a good job of managing those activities that go into making them.*

People at all levels of a company make decisions every day that affect the firm's success. And who are the people who have more impact than anybody else on everything that happens in any company, including yours? The managers. Thus, to the extent that employees tend to make decisions that advance or harm the company's interests, much of the credit or blame must fall squarely on the shoulders of the managers. Day in and day out, managers take actions, wittingly and unwittingly, that determine how and how well the people around them decide. Collectively, these actions constitute *decision management.*

Managers universally recognize their responsibility to make good decisions. But relatively few understand that to be a manager is necessarily also to be a *decision* manager. It is obvious that Borders could have made a better decision in hiring a new CEO. It is harder to recognize that the chances of making such a decision would have been dramatically improved if better decision managers had been on the scene.

This is not to say that decision management is only about preventing blunders. A company that avoids big mistakes may well survive—yet still be eclipsed by more imaginative competitors. Good decision management can not only reduce the odds of disaster but also increase the chances of spectacularly effective decisions.

Simply put, the purpose of this book is to help you become a great decision manager, someone who improves the odds that the people you influence will make decisions that enhance the prosperity of your company. Like all management, decision management is an art, but one that can be informed by a knowledge of scientific principles and a body of both research and practical experience.

The remainder of this chapter introduces what decision management involves and how you can better fulfill your obligation as a manager to improve the decision processes in your area of responsibility. Along the way, I will sketch the book's strategy for helping you develop your decision management expertise and offer some first suggestions for developing your own strategy for improving the decision making in your company.

■ The Decision Management Portfolio

Decision management encompasses all the things that every manager does, consciously or otherwise, that damage or improve the quality of the company's decisions, and thereby the company's welfare. Clearly, managers have countless ways to affect the decision making of the people within their circles of influence. Fortunately, decision management activities can be sorted usefully into four categories, as shown in Figure 1.1. You can view these categories as your portfolio of decision management responsibilities or, even better, as your portfolio of opportunities—opportunities to help make decision making a pillar of strength for the company. The upcoming sections discuss each opportunity in turn.

The Decision Management Portfolio

Influencing Specific Decisions

- Deciding personally
- Participating in decision groups
- Affecting others' decision deliberations

Supervising Decision Routines

Shaping Decision Practices

Providing Decision Resources

Figure 1.1. The Portfolio of Decision Management Responsibilities or Opportunities

Influencing Specific Decisions

Decision managers influence some specific company decisions relatively directly. This happens in three ways.

First, like every employee, managers make some company decisions personally. Managers' decisions are special in that the higher the rank of the manager the more consequential the decisions become.

Second, managers typically are members of many different groups that have extraordinary decision authority. So, for example, an accounting manager might be part of a cross-functional team planning a new product as well as a member of the finance division's standing compensation committee. Although the individual managers do not have the power to make decisions outside their own spheres on their own, they share in the group decisions.

The third way that managers influence specific decisions is deceptively powerful—by having effects on other people's deliberations. Bring to mind virtually any serious decision problem that was charged to some group of people in your company, say, a CEO search committee. Though the group made the ultimate decision collectively, some people in the group exerted more influence on the decision than others. Suppose, for instance, that you were chairing the group. Then, in subtle and perhaps not-so-subtle ways, you had a heavy hand in shaping the process that produced the final decision, for example, by hiring and supervising support staff, scheduling and drafting the agenda of each meeting, and directing the flow of discussion, such as cutting off long-winded discussants and soliciting the thoughts of reticent ones. Of course, the other members of a decision group can also influence the process, and hence the outcome, in any number of ways. For example, any member who wishes to do so can help direct the flow of discussion ("We haven't heard what Jake thinks yet. So, what's on your mind, Jake?"), suggest alternatives ("Have you folks thought of Brenda Lake over at Imperial?"), or offer decision-relevant information ("Why don't you take a look at this report I ran across?")—all activities that have a direct bearing on others' deliberations and consequently on the quality of the group's decision.

Supervising Decision Routines

Every company has routines—even if only informal ones—for making decisions of various kinds, particularly recurrent decisions. Sometimes these routines are executed at the personal level, at other times collaboratively. For example, every bookstore chain has rules that its store managers must follow when they hire clerks. And most chains probably have developed customs if not written procedures for deciding which new books they will carry, procedures that rest on the opinions of several individuals. As a manager, you are involved in designing and assuring the smooth functioning of routines like these all the time. You must also determine when those rules need to be revised and must then see that the improvements are actually put in place. This, too, is decision management.

Like all aspects of company culture, decision customs often differ sharply from one company to the next. Clashes in customs like these are a key reason that mergers and acquisitions seem to fail at least as often as they succeed. For instance, some analysts have argued that such clashes were a major contributor to the rough going experienced in DaimlerChrysler's efforts to create a successful integrated business from the previously independent Daimler Benz and Chrysler companies. They have noted that the German decision style prevalent at Daimler Benz (a highly formal one) clashed sharply with the style at Chrysler (which was more flexible and freewheeling).[2] Cases like this give us a further reason to pay close attention not only to what decisions get made, but also the routines that produce those decisions.

Shaping Decision Practices

We affect and are affected by almost everybody around us. Thus, as a result of their interactions with you, the people who come into contact with you do things differently than they did before. As a manager, however, you are in an unusually strong position to influence other people's behavior, including how they make decisions.

Some of that influence is transitory, as when you reward behavior with incentives. The influence of incentives tends to fade once you stop consistently rewarding a particular behavior. Other influences are longer lasting, resulting in new customs that largely sustain themselves. People acquire many enduring customs and habits by observing and imitating those around them, especially those (like managers) who serve as models for them. As most parents discover, often to their sorrow, the example we set without realizing it is often more powerful than our deliberate attempts to instruct others—no matter how often anyone says, "Do as I say," the result is that others "Do as I do." As a manager, then, you shape decision practices—for good or ill—by the way you go about making decisions. And to the extent that you influence the way decisions are generally made, you have a hand in shaping a culture of decision making that works to either the advantage or the disadvantage of your company.

Providing Decision Resources

The decision procedures people use are one constraint on the quality of the decisions they make. Another key constraint is the resources people have available when making their decisions. These resources include the personnel at their disposal as well as the tools they can apply to decision problems, for instance, their computers and software. Another—and critical—resource is time. As a primary care physician in a major health system put it to me, "Time is my biggest problem. I have to be honest with you. In the fourteen minutes the health plan allows me with each patient, I cannot even *talk* to the patient about all of the treatment and prevention options that advocates insist we simply *'must'* offer to every patient."

One of your standard responsibilities as a manager is allocating resources. That applies to your role as a *decision* manager as well. Good decision management in this respect means exercising the sensitivity and skill required to ensure that people have the resources they need to make effective decisions while at the same time avoiding wasting resources that could be used better elsewhere.

■ Drivers of Poor Decision Management

The four categories of activity in the decision management portfolio give you an overview of the ways in which you can influence your company's decisions for the better. Becoming conscious of this portfolio of opportunities is a first step toward becoming a better decision manager. A second step is to be aware of the hazards that often impede good decision management so that you can steer clear of them.

Picture chef Jordan Lynx, who is highly accomplished but has always had trouble preparing one important dish—coq au vin. Eventually fed up with his coq au vin failures, Lynx solicits the help of good friend and fellow chef Traci Moore, whose coq au vin wins awards. Moore tells Lynx: "OK, Jordan, why don't we start by just letting me watch you make it the way you normally do?" After this exercise, Moore says: "This is going to be easy, my friend. Your technique is fundamentally sound. But I can see that there're just a few specific, 'little' things you're doing wrong that make all the difference in the world. So, let's get those things fixed, OK?" Then off they go, and before you know it, Lynx's coq au vin is a winner.

This book's strategy for helping you become a first-class decision manager is largely the same as the one Traci Moore used in helping Jordan Lynx with his coq au vin. Research and experience have shown that when managers fall short as *decision* managers, it is typically because of a small number of specific things that they do or fail to do. So let me describe four key drivers of decision management difficulties, with a view toward how they will be addressed throughout the book.

Driver 1: Failure to Recognize Responsibility

Many managers are oblivious to the impact that their actions (and sometimes inactions) have on the people around them, including all four of the classes of decision management actions just discussed. In effect, these managers fail to recognize that decision management is one of their responsibilities or, alternatively, opportunities to provide invaluable service for their companies (and their careers). Little wonder, then, that they do an inadequate job of fulfilling those duties; they are not even trying to fulfill them. By simply becoming aware of decision management as a core managerial responsibility, you will be ahead of the game.

Driver 2: Vague Appreciation for Decision Problems and Processes

At a superficial level, everyone understands what hitting a golf ball entails. ("You just swing that stick, right?") At a similar level of superficiality, everybody knows what decision problems are and what solving them entails. Unfortunately, superficial understanding typically is insufficient for guiding intelligent and effective efforts to either strike golf balls or manage decisions. Also unfortunately, all too often, managers have no more than a vague grasp of the true nature of decision problems and processes. Throughout this book, you will be thoroughly immersed in careful analyses of what decision problems entail and what is required to solve them.

Driver 3: Ignorance of Natural Decision Making

When a mechanic sets out to repair your car, it obviously helps if he understands how and why cars like yours work generally— or not. And it *really* helps if he understands why your *particular* car is acting up. By the same token, a decision manager is handicapped if she does not understand how and why people in general tend to decide the way they do naturally. She is at a marked disadvantage if she is clueless about what is peculiar about how the people in her own company decide.

From the perspective used in this book, an understanding of how people decide reduces to an understanding of how they address each of the ten cardinal decision issues introduced in the next section. These ten issues are a way of conceptualizing the chain of activities that lead to an ultimate decision. Throughout the book, you will become acquainted with essential findings from the scientific literature about how people generally tend to deal with these issues and how you can get a fix on the ways the particular people in your corner of the company tend to handle them.

Driver 4: Limited Awareness of Useful Principles

Unlike, say, accounting, finance, logistics, or some marketing functions, expertise in decision management does not rest on mastering a prescribed set of procedures or routines. Instead, it demands creative and adaptive improvisation in situations that exhibit the messy but fascinating variety and fluidity of everyday life.

This does not mean, however, that anything goes or that becoming an expert decision manager is an unteachable matter of chance. Another analogy is apt. To the naive observer, theatrical improvisation (as practiced, for instance, by the Second City comedy troupe in Chicago) seems chaotic and haphazard. Actually, though, theatrical improvisers learn and imaginatively apply principles that have proved their worth over many years. In a similar way, imaginative decision managers can make use of principles developed from both research and practical experience.

■ The Ten Cardinal Decision Issues

Individual managers sometimes accidentally discover the basic principles of decision management for themselves. But this is unacceptably chancy and inefficient. That is why this book details a number of the most important and useful principles that can guide your efforts to improve decision making in your company.

As I have already noted, becoming an outstanding decision manager requires developing a deep appreciation for what decision problems and processes really involve. In Chapter Two, I will give you a closer look at decision problems. Here I want to flesh out the practical meaning of *decision processes.*

Careful study has shown that, in some form or another, almost every practical decision problem poses each of the ten fundamental or *cardinal* decision issues listed in Table 1.1. From this perspective, we can define "decision processes" as *ways that deciders go about resolving the cardinal decision issues as they arise in the decision problems that confront them.* Since the mission of decision managers is to maintain and constantly improve their companies' decision processes, we can formulate this mission as follows:

> The decision manager's task is to do whatever
> it takes to ensure that the deciders in the company
> do a good job of resolving the ten cardinal issues
> for every decision problem that comes along.

How, specifically, you can fulfill this mission is the subject of the rest of this book. In particular, Chapters Three through Eight provide a detailed discussion all ten cardinal issues. The following preview conveys the gist of each issue, in the voice of deciders who are confronted with it and with a real-life example:

- Issue 1: Need. *Why are we (not) deciding anything at all?* Example: How did it come to the attention of Coca-Cola's leadership that the company had the problem that their ill-fated decision to introduce New Coke was intended to solve? (Had they never recognized the problem, they never would have made—and regretted—the decision.)
- Issue 2: Mode. *Who (or what) will make this decision, and how will they approach that task?* Example: How will it be determined who will recommend and choose the next chairman of Goldman Sachs?
- Issue 3: Investment. *What kinds and amounts of resources will be invested in the process of making this decision?* Example: Ford

Table 1.1. **The Ten Cardinal Decision Issues**

Issue	Description
1. Need	Why are we (not) deciding anything at all?
2. Mode	Who (or what) will make this decision, and how will they approach that task?
3. Investment	What kinds and amounts of resources will be invested in the process of making this decision?
4. Options	What are the different actions we could potentially take to deal with this problem we have?
5. Possibilities	What are the various things that could potentially happen if we took that action—things they care about?
6. Judgment	Which of the things that they care about actually *would* happen if we took that action?
7. Value	How much would they *really* care—positively or negatively—if that in fact happened?
8. Tradeoffs	All of our prospective actions have both strengths and weaknesses. So how should we make the tradeoffs that are required to settle on the action we will actually pursue?
9. Acceptability	How can we get them to agree to this decision and this decision procedure?
10. Implementation	That's what we decided to do. Now, how can we get it done, or *can* we get it done, after all?

Motor Company has seemingly countless suppliers. Does it spend too much time and money choosing those suppliers— or too little?

- Issue 4: Options. *What are the different actions we could potentially take to deal with this problem we have?* Example: When Boeing was facing the problem of where to relocate its headquarters, it considered only certain cities. Why? Should it have considered others?

- Issue 5: Possibilities. *What are the various things that could potentially happen if we took that action—things they care about?* In the language of Chapter Two, the "they" in this question refers to the decision's beneficiaries and stakeholders. Example: A local public organization negotiated substantial signing bonuses for members of one of its unions. Only later did the board realize that "me too" (benefits-matching) clauses in other contracts obliged it to pay hundreds of thousands of dollars to its other unions as well. Why did the board completely overlook this possibility before approving the contract?

- Issue 6: Judgment. *Which of the things that they care about actually would happen if we took that action?* Example: A Borders official attributed Phil Pfeffer's difficulties as the company's CEO to his not being "a good fit" with the company.[3] Why did the Borders board of directors fail to recognize this before Pfeffer was hired?

- Issue 7: Value. *How much would they really care—positively or negatively—if that in fact happened?* Example: The managers at a service facility were worried about rising personnel costs. They therefore sought to reduce their older staff by about half. So they crafted a buyout plan and offered it to employees beyond a certain level of seniority. To their surprise, virtually *all* the eligible employees took the buyout, leaving the facility so badly understaffed that they had to hire expensive contract workers to fill in. Why were the managers so far out of touch with the older employees' feelings, their values?

- Issue 8: Tradeoffs. *All of our prospective actions have both strengths and weaknesses. So how should we make the tradeoffs that are required to settle on the action we will actually pursue?* Example: The engineers at a major auto parts manufacturer had to choose between an old flange design and a new one that was stronger but required greater assembly time. Which consideration should have taken priority?

- Issue 9: Acceptability. *How can we get them to agree to this decision and this decision procedure?* Example: A local grocer decided to extend its hours to increase profits. To the surprise and dismay of the proprietors, the neighbors complained and threatened a boycott because of the resulting late-night commotion. What should the company have done to avoid this unfortunate turn of events?
- Issue 10: Implementation. *That's what we decided to do. Now, how can we get it done, or can we get it done, after all?* Example: The information technology director of a global manufacturer eagerly agreed to develop a product tracking system internally. Only later did he discover that his unit could not deliver. Why only then?

For each of these ten issues, facilitating better decision making involves being aware of how people usually resolve these issues, common errors that people make, countermeasures you can take to prevent these errors from occurring, and steps you can take to encourage exceptionally effective ways of resolving the issues. This book will give you principles and techniques that can help you ensure that the decision processes in your company work to produce the best decisions possible.

■ Your Strategy

I have just described the strategy of the book. But what about *your* strategy? What approach can you take to substantially improve the way people in your company make decisions? Here are some ideas that work.

Aggressively Pursue Opportunities

Successful decision managers are constantly and aggressively on the lookout for opportunities to improve how the company's people decide. The decision management portfolio in Figure 1.1 provides a good reminder of the opportunities available to you. "Influencing" and "Providing" opportunities are especially obvious when the company is faced with an unusually big decision, such as a strategy shift, a major product launch, or a change in compensation policies. "Supervising" and "Shaping" opportunities are easy to neglect because they do not hit you in the face with their urgency (despite their enormous significance, given that the pertinent decisions are so numerous). Instead, you must regularly, actively, and systematically examine decision routines and practices throughout your part of the company. For instance, suppose that you are heavily involved in supplier relations in the company. Then, as you go about your normal duties in that arena, you can constantly ask yourself questions like these: "How are we picking these suppliers? Couldn't we be doing better? How?"

Review the Ten Cardinal Issues

A straightforward, thorough, and reliable way to approach improving any decision-making process starts with the list of ten cardinal decision issues. For each issue in the list, ask yourself: "How are we naturally inclined to deal with this issue for this kind of problem? Is that *really* the best we can do?" You would then make the appraisal vis-à-vis the standards developed in the heart of this book. Often what people are already doing about an issue is good enough—that is, either sufficiently effective or at least not so far from optimal as to be worth the trouble of trying to change it. But the investment you make in examining how people in the company deal with each issue will be more than repaid by the times when you discover an opportunity to substantially improve on what they do. One reason this is so is that in many decision situations, people never even recognize that particular issues exist. This means that those issues must resolve themselves by chance or default. And that is unacceptably risky for your company.

Exploit Sound Principles

Throughout this book you will learn numerous principles that provide the basic logic for addressing the cardinal decision issues effectively. When you detect that the company's approach to an issue needs to be improved, review the relevant principles. They will provide a sensible starting point for your efforts.

Draw on Your Experience, Creativity, and Colleagues

The ideas in this book are only a starting point. You have three other critical sources of ideas for improving the handling of the cardinal decision issues on which you can—and indeed, *must*—draw.

The first source of ideas is the experience you have accumulated as a manager and as a member of your company. No outsider can possibly know vital particulars about your company as well as you do.

The second source is your creativity. For every decision management problem that presents itself, ask yourself, "What might work here?" As I will have occasion to note later in the book, each of us is capable of considerable creativity, especially if we pay attention to some of the factors known to facilitate that quality.

The final idea source is your colleagues (and *their* experience and creativity). There really is something to the old adage that "Two (or more) heads are better than one." As long as you observe the principles governing interpersonal collaborations discussed later in the book, you will be able to profit from the potential embodied in the people around you.

Create a Plan for Implementation

The best decision improvement ideas in the world would be utterly worthless if you failed to put them into action. Thus an absolutely essential element of your decision management strategy is to develop a workable plan for implementing any idea you come up with and for *sustaining* that implementation. Implementation requires lots of different things, one of which is skill at persuading other people to cooperate with you. Chapter Eight, which discusses the implementation issue, will provide further insight on this aspect of your strategy.

Anticipate and Deal with Resistance

The point about cooperation brings up a potentially serious hazard you will probably face as a decision manager. For the most part, decision management is about getting other people to decide better and hence differently than they did before. The problem is that people seldom eagerly embrace new ways of deciding. Indeed, more typically, they actively resist attempts to get them to decide differently. This can be highly discouraging for a decision manager. ("This is making everybody hate me," you may well think. "Why am I beating my head against this brick wall?") It is easy to just give up in the face of such opposition. You need to plan for resistance. Otherwise you will be sorely tempted to give up on your decision management efforts.

A big reason that people resist changing how they decide is that they see no need to do so. That is, people generally believe that their own decision making is just fine. They say things like, "I've been making decisions my whole career—my whole life—and I'm obviously doing OK, right? So why mess with a good thing?" Moreover, when they observe others making bad decisions, they tend to dismiss those incidents as holding no lessons for themselves. Suppose you were to describe the disastrous Borders CEO selection story to the leaders in your own company and then ask what it might mean for your company. Based on research findings (some of which I will discuss later), I would be willing to bet that they would say "Nothing," because they could not even imagine themselves making such an "obvious and silly" mistake.

A related reason for resistance to new ways of deciding is the enormous variety in the ways people decide naturally. When you step back and think about it, this variety makes a lot of sense. Consider other everyday behaviors, such as talking and eating. We each have our own styles of speaking and our own peculiar likes and dislikes in foods. These varied and deeply ingrained styles and tastes arise from the fact that from birth we have grown up in different households and have been exposed to and shaped by people with their own distinctive styles and tastes. The same is true of decision customs. So when someone comes along and says, "This is the right way to decide," people are understandably skeptical and even hostile. To a point, their skepticism is well founded. That is because for most of the tasks that must be accomplished to make a good decision, there really is no uniquely *right* way of achieving those tasks; any number of tacks could work.

So what should you do—and *not* do—about resistance? First of all, anticipate it. Expect people to be firmly wedded to their particular ways of deciding. Then try to uncover what their customs and preferences are. (I have seen skillful committee chairs do this by starting discussions with remarks like: "So, how do you folks think we ought to proceed?") Now, suppose that you detect flaws in what you discover. Probably the worst thing you could do is say, "That doesn't make sense" or "Let's do it this way instead" or anything along those lines. The resistance will be immediate and insurmountable. A wiser course is to negotiate a consensus about how the pertinent decision tasks will be accomplished, given the variety of opinions, including your own. With practice, you will develop your skills of gentle persuasion, making liberal use of comments such as: "I can see why you feel that way, but how about . . . ?"

Recruit Collaborators and Keep Their Eyes on the Payoff

Suppose that everybody within your circle of influence in the company is as committed to outstanding decision management as you are. That is, *everyone* is constantly seeking better ways of managing the company's decision processes. Then much of the resistance you would experience otherwise would simply not exist. More positively, your company's progress toward developing a "stellar decision management culture" would explode and sustain itself, largely without your continuing personal efforts. This is the ideal of all true leadership and should be your goal here.

How can you achieve this ideal? You must recruit collaborators in your decision management campaign. Start with the people in your immediate office as well as your closest peer managers. Then urge them to draw in others until the ambition of constantly improving decision management practices is simply a natural way of thinking throughout the company. To recruit these collaborators, you need to point to (and keep pointing to) the payoffs of better decision management for the company and for them personally. Right now, you have only an abstract promise of what those payoffs are. But by the time you are finished with this book, you will have seen many concrete illustrations, one after another, and will know where to find (and will create) many of your own. You will have no trouble citing familiar and compelling cases, as in observations like these: "Remember the Smith fiasco? There's virtually no chance that something like that could happen the way we deal with the possibilities issue these days."

CHAPTER SUMMARY

All managers are *decision managers.* That is, intentionally or not, they take actions that affect how and how well the people in their companies make decisions. From this perspective, decision management is a core managerial responsibility, but one too few managers recognize as such.

The portfolio of decision management activities includes influencing specific decisions, supervising decision routines, shaping decision practices, and providing decision resources. There are several reasons why decision management is often inadequate: managers do not recognize that they are responsible for managing their companies' decisions; they possess only a vague appreciation for the true character of decision problems and decision processes; there are significant gaps in their understanding of how people decide naturally; and they have only limited awareness of useful decision principles. In effect, this book mounts a concentrated attack on each of these drivers of poor decision management. The cornerstone of that attack is a characterization of decision processes as ways that deciders seek to resolve each of ten cardinal issues that arise in virtually all decision problems.

A manager's chances of improving decision processes are enhanced significantly if guided by a coherent strategy. Some key elements in such a strategy include aggressively pursuing decision improvement opportunities; drawing on one's experience, creativity, and colleagues; creating a plan for implementation; anticipating and dealing with resistance; and recruiting collaborators.

Questions for Consideration

1. Take a few moments to bring to mind managers with whom you have worked over the years. Which of those managers do you consider to have been the best *decision* manager? Label this manager *BDM,* for obvious reasons. Which of those individuals do you regard as the worst decision manager of the whole group? Call this person *WDM.*

   Now construct a small table. Label each row of the table with one of the four classes of activities in the decision management portfolio: influencing specific decisions, supervising decision routines, shaping decision practices, and providing decision resources. Label one column of the table BDM. In each cell in that column, briefly note an incident that best illustrates how BDM approaches the given decision management activity. For instance, in the influence row of that column, note a prototypical instance in which BDM took actions that significantly affected how several people collaboratively made a decision that had major consequences for your company. In another column of the table, record reminders of similar incidents for WDM.

When you are done with your table, simply reflect on it. Ask yourself questions like these: "What's different about how BDM and WDM manage decisions? Why do they do things so differently? Suppose I were supervising both BDM and WDM. How could I get WDM to function more like BDM?"

2. What was, in your view, the worst decision made in your office within the past year? Now consider each of the ten cardinal decision issues sketched in this chapter. Which one of those issues was most critical in the sense that the deciders' mishandling of that issue was most responsible for the decision turning out so badly? What did the deciders' bosses do—or fail to do—that was, in turn, most responsible for the deciders' ineffectiveness?

"What Is a Decision?" and Other Fundamentals

Centuries ago, a Chinese prince called upon the sage
Confucius for help with a highly practical problem—how
to reform the government.

"What will you consider the first thing to be done?" asked
Tzu-lu, who conveyed the prince's request.

Confucius replied, "What is necessary is to rectify names."

"So, indeed!" exclaimed Tzu-lu. "You are wide of the
mark. Why must there be such rectification?"

Confucius answered, "How uncultivated you are! A
superior man, in regard to what he does not know, shows
a cautious reserve. If names be not correct, language is not
in accordance with the truth of things. If language be not in
accordance with the truth of things, affairs cannot be carried
on to success."[1]

This chapter reflects that ancient wisdom. Becoming a good decision manager requires thinking more precisely about the language of decisions than people ordinarily do. To convince yourself of this point, try a simple experiment. Ask a half dozen of your colleagues to define what a decision is. Then ask them to define what a *good* decision is. I would be willing to bet that you will get a variety of answers, with a good deal of fuzziness in the bargain.

Variety and fuzziness may not matter much in everyday conversation, but they become crucial when we want to apply sound principles in improving decision processes. For that purpose, we need to be as clear and precise about the meaning of our core terminology as an accountant is about such concepts as assets and liabilities. And we need to ensure that, so far as possible, our language is "in accordance with the truth of things."

This chapter therefore defines the fundamental concepts needed to explore decision processes in detail. It also provides you with the start of the toolkit you need as a decision manager.

It begins with the most fundamental question of all: What is a decision?

■ Decisions

This is what the term *decision* will mean here:

> A decision is a commitment to an action that
> is intended to yield satisfying states of affairs for
> particular parties, called the *beneficiaries* of that action.

This formal definition is probably a little more elaborate than one you would write yourself, but it is essentially a composite of how people use the term *decision* in practice. Each of its key elements will prove to be significant in the discussion of decision processes, so it is worthwhile to expand on them just a bit.

Commitment to Action

Decisions express a resolve to take a particular action. The action in question should be distinguished from the decision itself. A decision is made when the decider or deciders commit to a definite course. Suppose, for example, that Sharon Block, the chair of the hiring committee, confirms the consensus of the committee and says, "So, Rodriguez gets the offer, right?" Then and there, the decision to hire Rodriguez has occurred, even though the offer has not yet been tendered or accepted.

Intention

Decision making is deliberate. People decide purposefully, to achieve specific ends; they do not decide by accident, although particular elements of decision processes sometimes become nonconscious and therefore occasionally problematic. When Jim began screening credit applications for Majestic Appliances five years ago, it made sense to pay attention to employment within the city. Since then, however, local demographics have changed and that screen no longer helps Jim distinguish good from poor credit risks. Nevertheless, he still takes city residence into account despite trying not to do so; he cannot help himself.

Satisfaction for Beneficiaries

All decisions have beneficiaries whose interests the decision is intended to serve. People sometimes make decisions solely on their own behalf, as when they choose between two available work spaces. In such cases, the deciders themselves are the targeted beneficiaries. And even when people make decisions on behalf of other beneficiaries, they cannot help trying to serve their own interests as well. When a unit manager decides on work assignments for her staff, she is making a decision for her unit and company, and perhaps for the staff members as well, but one of her considerations undoubtedly will be how the resulting quality of work will reflect on her as a leader. ("I don't think Dave can do that. And if he doesn't, what would *I* look like?")

Almost by definition, however, the typical business decision is one the decider makes mainly on behalf of others. So, for instance, when the designers at Advanced Apparel choose what will and will not go into the company's new spring children's line, their choices are primarily intended to please a certain class of beneficiaries—the company's potential customers.

The idea of satisfaction implies a key point about what often makes decision making so difficult, compared to other forms of problem solving: people vary widely in their likes and dislikes—their values. When we solve a calculus problem, a correct solution is simply a correct solution—for everybody. Decision problems are different. When Burt is faced with picking out a new outfit for his daughter Ashley, the new Advanced Apparel jumper may be an ideal solution to him. ("Wow, this looks great!") Yet the same choice might repel another customer who is faced with exactly the same problem for his little girl. Decision makers thus face the complication that the right answer for one beneficiary may not be the right answer for another. And the situation is further complicated because beneficiaries are not the only parties to a decision.

■ Types of Decisions

The discussion so far characterizes decisions generally, but it's possible to be even more precise by recognizing that decisions come in four distinct types, each with its own special features and demands.

Type 1: choice decisions. In choice decisions, the decider is faced with two or more discrete, specified alternatives and must choose a subset from that pool, perhaps just one of those options. A site example: "So does the new plant go to Amsterdam or to Bonn?" When most people think about what qualifies as a decision, choices are what come to mind immediately.

Type 2: accept/reject decisions. In accept/reject decisions, the decider is presented with one option only and must either take it or leave it. An investment illustration: "Should we replace the Number 5 press?" A proposal example: "Does this acquisition of Leung Services make sense for us?" Accept/reject decisions are a special case of choice decisions in that the decider actually has two options, taking the offered alternative or refusing to do so.

Type 3: evaluation decisions. In evaluation decisions, the decider must commit to a course of action based on an assessment of the worth of some entity, that is, on an evaluation. A bidding example: "Should we, as our analysis says, submit a quote of $35 million on that highway rehabilitation project?" A performance appraisal illustration: "Should I give Marie an 8 out of 10 this year?"

Type 4: construction decisions. In construction decisions, the decider must use available resources to try to assemble the ideal alternative, subject to particular constraints. A budgeting illustration: "Our total available funds come to $50 million. The proposed budget for sales is $7 million, for manufacturing $22 million, [and so on]. Is this the budget we should approve?" A negotiations example: "Here's where we are. . . . Have we finally come up with a package that both sides can live with?"

■ Decision Parties

As the examples so far suggest, business decisions are unlike many other kinds of problems in that they are often intricate social affairs. They involve a variety of parties whose differing values and interests are in some way affected by the decision. In fact, in nearly every significant situation that arises, good decision making demands an acute awareness of exactly who the key parties are, what matters to them, how they are likely to behave, and what effects their actions are likely to have. Figure 2.1 sketches the major categories of parties we must recognize for any decision.

Beneficiaries

First of all, there are the decision's beneficiaries, the people whose interests the decision is expressly intended to serve. Figure 2.1 distinguishes two categories of these beneficiaries: distant and immediate.

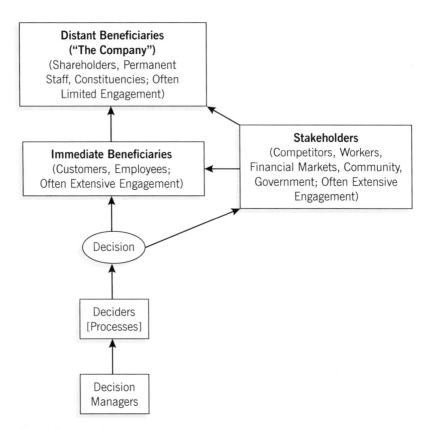

Figure 2.1. Decision Parties

Primary among distant beneficiaries are people who have made investments of various kinds in the company and whose ends the company was established to achieve. For the most part, when we speak of "the company," as in "serving the company's welfare," these are the people who are in mind. They include the owners, such as shareholders. They also often include long-term employees who have committed much of their lives to the company, and also the constituencies companies frequently say they are committed to serving, such as the sick in the case of a drug manufacturer.

Distant beneficiaries are distant in two senses. First, they often have no day-to-day involvement with the company's activities. People who own shares through their unions' pension funds are an extreme example. Second, distant beneficiaries' interests ordinarily are not served directly by any specific company decision. Instead, other steps must occur in between, steps involving immediate decision beneficiaries.

The typical company decision is intended to serve the concrete needs and interests of specific groups of people. That is why it makes sense to call these people *immediate* beneficiaries. Their actions in turn eventually create or destroy the economic value that is often the sole concern of distant beneficiaries such as shareholders. Consumers and employees are the best examples of immediate beneficiaries. If few customers want the products that managers choose to introduce to the market, the company's sales will generate meager profits for the owners. And if the managers' investment decisions leave their workers with antiquated equipment that cripples their productivity, then there obviously will be little to try to sell.

Deciders and Decision Managers

Then there are, of course, the deciders. For the moment, the important thing to realize is that the deciders reach their decisions by means of their decision processes, their own particular ways of addressing the cardinal decision issues introduced in Chapter One. It is through these processes that another class of parties to a decision, the decision managers, noted at the bottom of Figure 2.1, has an impact on what is ultimately decided. As suggested by the plural "managers," for the typical consequential business decision, several decision managers play roles, not just one.

Stakeholders

The final category of decision parties consists of the stakeholders for a given decision. Stakeholders are people who have two qualifications. The first is that they are, or could be, affected by the decision, even though, in contrast to beneficiaries, serving their interests is not a goal of the deciders. The second qualification is that stakeholders have power and are likely to exercise it to affect the company's interests if they are pleased or, more likely, displeased by the decision. In Figure 2.1, that power is represented by the arrows from the stakeholders to the beneficiaries. Stakeholders are appropriately acknowledged this way because their actions can enhance or diminish the beneficiaries' "satisfying states of affairs," which are the aims of the deciders.

Competitors are an inescapable class of stakeholders. Clearly, their responses to any company decision are critical to the company's success. In the case of public corporations, financial markets—that is, professionals such as analysts as well as potential investors—are key stakeholders, too. Their mere beliefs about the wisdom of a decision—well founded or not—can cause share prices to skyrocket or plunge in a flash. To the extent that their efforts are required to carry out a decision, regardless of whether the decision was intended to serve their personal interests, a company's employees are stakeholders also. After all, if the employees believe that the decision harms their interests, they might well seek to thwart it.

Classic examples of bystander stakeholders are the neighbors surrounding a company's facilities. Note that, like immediate decision beneficiaries (and unlike many distant benefici-aries), stakeholders often have extensive, even unavoidable, en-gagement with a company. Their stakes can be very high indeed, as when a company pollutes its neighbors' ground water. ("You criminals are killing my kids!")

It is important to recognize that for any single decision problem, the same person can belong to more than one of the categories just described. For instance, as a member of a com-mittee on compensation, you might play the role of decision manager at the same time that you are serving as one of the de-ciders. And as an employee of the company, you are a benefici-ary as well. Thus the various decision parties represent roles rather than particular individuals, and these roles can shift from one decision to the next and even from one phase of a decision episode to another.

■ Quality

As a decision manager, your responsibility is to see that people in your company decide well. Exercising this responsibility re-quires that you do things such as clean up the mess after disas-trous decisions, replace poor deciders, and train new, better ones. At the heart of each of these actions and, indeed, decision making itself, is the notion of quality—decision quality, decision process quality, and decider quality. What exactly should these ideas mean, and how should you, as a decision manager, make them functional in practice?

Decision Quality

This is what the term *effective decision* will mean here:

> An effective decision is a decision that results in
> satisfying states of affairs for its intended beneficiaries.

The qualifier *effective* is appropriate because it implies that a decision achieves the purpose implicit in the definition of *decision*. I pointedly recommend using this term rather than *good decision* because the latter expression is ambiguous and brings with it too much excess baggage from everyday usage as well as controversies among decision scholars.

This broad characterization of effective decisions is fine as far as it goes, but it is less precise than what you need in many real-life decision management situations. In particular, it fails to acknowledge the more specific standards of decision quality that most people, including clients and superiors, clearly recognize and demand that deciders achieve. Recognition of those quality dimensions would therefore provide you with more concrete targets that focus your efforts to improve decisions in your company. This leads to the following practical version of the definition of an effective decision:

> An effective decision is a decision that is strong
> with respect to aim, need, aggregated outcomes,
> rival options, and process costs criteria.

It's worth looking at what these criteria entail.

The aim criterion. Deciders make decisions in order to accomplish quite specific things, their aims, whether they explicitly articulate those aims to other people or not. That is:

> A decision is strong with respect to the aim criterion
> if it achieves the aims that the deciders set for that decision.

Every decider I have ever known considers a decision to have failed to the extent that it falls short of realizing its aims. Thus, when Borders chose Phil Pfeffer as its new CEO, its board probably intended for the appointment to improve the company's share prices, among other things, and was disappointed when it did not.

The need criterion. As the ideas will be developed in Chapter Three, a company can have either of two kinds of needs: calamity-focused or opportunity-focused. When a company has a *calamity-focused* need, this means that, if the company were to continue its present course, it would encounter forces that seriously damage its interests. Many automobile executives, for instance, see the industry's worldwide overcapacity as a reality that will cripple if not destroy their companies if they continue business as usual. Ideally, every auto company should make decisions that meet the implied need. When a company has an *opportunity-focused* need, this means that there are conditions which, if properly exploited, will benefit the company. Suppose a company is well established in a community that has a growing population of wealthy older adults. That demographic trend constitutes an opportunity the company can use to its advantage by providing products and services elderly people demand. Decisions to do so would serve the implied need. More generally:

> A decision has strength with respect to the
> need criterion to the extent that it meets important
> needs that the company actually possesses.

An important observation: Deciders invariably aspire to have their aims coincide with real, significant needs that their companies have. Thus deciders typically begin a decision episode with what they perceive to be specific needs that are bearing down on the company. They then establish as aims for their decisions the satisfaction of those needs. But two interesting situations at opposite extremes can arise, which highlight the value of acknowledging the need criterion:

- *The nil extreme: The deciders' aim does not correspond to an actual important need, nor does the decision serve any other significant company need.* Imagine, for example, that the leaders of Greene/Jeffers mistakenly believe that another company is about to launch a strong competitor to their flagship product and therefore decide to enter an alliance with a third firm. The decision achieves the deciders' aim of protecting the flagship product from the competing product, but the competing product—and hence the need for protection—never actually existed. The decision was pointless.

- *The positive extreme: The decision serves important company needs regardless of whether those needs were acknowledged as aims by the deciders.* Perhaps by accident, a decision might just happen to fully exploit a significant opportunity or preclude an impending disaster. Such was the case when a regional telecommunications equipment contractor hired a technologically naive young woman as a secretary in its main office. She performed that role just fine. But what was most remarkable is that she took it upon herself to learn the business inside and out and to develop solid relationships with the company's clients and staff. When the company's field manager resigned, leaving the company in a horrible bind, she was able to step right in as his replacement, despite her lack of formal credentials.

The aggregated outcomes criterion. Typically, once a decision is enacted, a multitude of things happen over time that affect the beneficiaries' interests, some of which bear on the deciders' aims for the decision, but the great majority of which usually do not. Some of these aim-independent outcomes serve the beneficiaries' interests while others harm them. The "aggregated outcomes" criterion reflects the net impact of all of a decision's consequences, positive and otherwise. Thus:

A decision is strong according to the aggregated outcomes criterion if the beneficiaries are highly satisfied with all the outcomes of the decision, taken as a whole.

This criterion figures especially prominently in personnel decisions. Consider a decision to hire a staff assistant. Even if the assistant meets the specifications of the job description perfectly, he brings with him all the variety of any real, live person— good and bad. He does work-related things that both delight and annoy you. The same goes for his personal habits and quirks. The resulting package leaves you generally pleased or displeased.

The rival options criterion. Imagine that you have just negotiated a complex supply contract with Schulz Manufacturing, with terms for all kinds of details, from unit price to delivery time to future options. The contract fulfills every objective (that is, aim) your company had going into the negotiations. It even provides lots of extras, heading off problems no one had any inkling were headed your way. You are, understandably, ecstatic about the deal. A day later, you learn that you could have had exactly the same contract with Davis Products except for one detail: Davis would have charged 10 percent less for every unit. Do you care? Of course you do. You no longer feel on top of the world, despite the fact that, on objective grounds, the Schulz deal is just as good as it was the day before. This situation provides a good illustration of the following notion:

> A decision is strong in terms of the rival options
> criterion if the state of affairs for each beneficiary is at
> least as good overall as it would have been had
> any other available option been selected.

The process costs criterion. Suppose that Decision A and Decision B produce identical outcomes, but it took fewer resources to arrive at Decision A. Every manager I know would say that Decision A was a better decision. Implicit is the following idea:

> A decision is strong in terms of the process
> costs criterion if the process of making that decision
> consumes minimal amounts of resources, such as money,
> time, and the deciders' capacity to endure aggravation.

Thus suppose that your operating committee spends an entire weekend wrangling over what to do about the East End facility and eventually decides to close it. All else being the same, this decision would be worse than the same decision arrived at in a single two-hour meeting on Wednesday afternoon.

You should recognize the distinction between *decision process costs* and *decision enactment costs.* The latter are the costs that would be incurred if a particular option were selected and enacted. For most of us, $200 would be lot of money to spend on a single bottle of wine at dinner. That is, the decision enactment costs in this case would be prodigious. For that very reason, it may take only an instant's deliberation to reject that option, meaning that our decision process costs are next to nil. Yet some diners (perhaps because they are wine connoisseurs) might just as quickly make the opposite choice, experiencing equally negligible decision process costs while incurring $200 in decision enactment costs.

Many people have a hard time appreciating the difference between decision process costs and decision enactment costs. The distinction has great importance for decision management purposes, so make sure that you have a firm grasp on it.

Decision Process Quality

It is useful to understand the characteristics of effective decisions, but that's not enough to maintain effective decision making. As a decision manager, your main concern is with the quality of the processes the people in your company employ when they make decisions. It is by influencing those processes (for instance, routines for reviewing job applicants) that you will seek to improve your company's decision making. So what defines *quality* with respect to decision processes? Simply this:

> A decision process is a good one to the extent
> that it tends to produce effective decisions, that is,
> ones that are strong with respect to the aim, need, aggregated
> outcomes, rival options, and process costs criteria.

The idea is the same as that entailed in manufacturing process control. Suppose that 960 of every 1000 tires produced by Process A are good while 980 of every 1000 produced by Process B meet that standard. Everyone would concede that Process B is the better process. Generalized to the case of decisions, notice that the definition just provided gives you a very specific and unambiguous characterization of what a good process is. The chapters to come will build on this idea.

Decider Quality

In your role as a decision manager, you also need to appraise the quality of deciders. Imagine that your boss asks you to recommend one of your staff for a highly sensitive project and insists: "Be sure to give me somebody who's a good decision maker." Do you send your boss Teresa or Daphne? Since a decider is, in essence, a human embodiment of a decision process, the same basic quality conception applies:

> A decider is good to the extent that he or she
> tends to produce effective decisions, ones that are
> strong with respect to the aim, need, aggregated outcomes,
> rival options, and process costs criteria.

So you would assign Teresa to your boss's project only if, on average, her decisions have been at least as effective as Daphne's, and preferably more so.

Quality Assessment Challenges

Having good conceptions of quality is indispensable. But you also need concrete means of assessing quality in specific situations. Assessing the effectiveness of any particular decision is straightforward—even if it is sometimes tedious and difficult to collect the required information. Suppose you needed to appraise the effectiveness of your company's decision to acquire another company. You would review your company's aims for the acquisition (including, perhaps, achieving a certain level of manufacturing capacity) and then determine whether the acquisition actually met those aims. You would then do something similar for the need, aggregated outcomes, rival options, and process costs criteria. Suppose that a person in your charge makes a grossly ineffective decision, for instance, one that loses a great deal of money for your company. Many managers would be tempted to discipline, even dismiss, that person. But some would reject such sanctions as inappropriate (and unfair) because chance often plays a significant role in decision outcomes. This argument has some validity. That is why it makes more sense to call a decider to task only when the decider employs a bad process. This therefore puts a premium on your ability to assess the quality of decision processes. As I noted before, in principle, you would make this assessment by examining many different decisions made via that process. You would pronounce the process *good* to the extent that the percentage of effective decisions is high, relying on the same statistical principles that engineers use in process control.

Unfortunately, in many business decision situations, accumulating large numbers of cases is simply not in the cards. For instance, it would be impossible to statistically assess the quality of a company's procedures for picking CEOs because the company chooses CEOs only rarely. Moreover, the selection procedures constantly change.

The cardinal decision issue perspective provides you with a way out. Suppose you need a means of judging whether the current CEO selection procedure is likely to yield an effective decision. You should examine how the procedure resolves each of the ten cardinal issues introduced in Chapter One. As shown in the remainder of the book, quite a lot is known about what are better and worse ways of settling those issues.

The Big Picture

As you go about your decision management mission, it will help to keep in mind a coherent picture of how everything fits together. I recommend constructing a mental image similar to the one in Figure 2.2. At the top is the ultimate objective, improving your company's welfare. At the bottom are the decision management options you will use to advance this objective. As the diagram shows, these actions achieve their effects through their influence on the ways people resolve the ten cardinal decision issues. Those resolutions in turn yield decisions that, ideally, improve the outcomes for the beneficiaries of the decisions.

■ Tools

Good managers are always on the lookout for tools they can adapt to the needs in their companies. (They often invent their own tools, too.) As a decision manager, you can add two devices to your toolkit immediately—cardinal issue checklists and causal factor analysis.

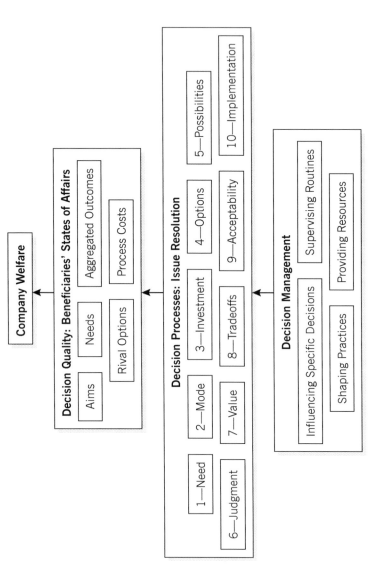

Figure 2.2. The Big Picture

Cardinal Issue Checklists

Since a good decision process is one that successfully resolves the ten cardinal decision issues, it is highly useful to have a checklist of these issues handy when you are evaluating or seeking to improve a given decision process. Otherwise, it is all too likely that one or more of the cardinal issues will be overlooked. Suppose that a group charged with selecting a new CEO is inattentive to Cardinal Issue 5, the possibilities issue. ("What are the various things that could potentially happen if we took that action—things they care about?") Such a group will probably be less inclined than otherwise to spontaneously ask questions like this: "What nonobvious things about this candidate could create problems for us down the road?" Failure to consider this issue would expose the group to a significant risk of selecting a candidate who fits poorly with the company. More generally, when deciders are oblivious to particular issues, the issues essentially resolve themselves by chance—with all the hazards that that entails. This kind of neglect is an enormously powerful reason that many business decisions fail.

Cardinal issue checklists provide protection against this kind of process failure. Checklists are adaptable to all four of your areas of decision management responsibility: influencing specific decisions, supervising decision routines, shaping decision practices, and providing decision resources. As you strive to fulfill your various decision management roles, referring to a list of the cardinal issues will prompt you to address each and every issue before concluding that a particular decision process is up to snuff.

Causal Factor Analysis

Causal factor analysis (CFA) is a family of techniques that investigators use to determine the causes of disasters such as airliner crashes and industrial accidents. You have undoubtedly seen news accounts of causal factor analyses after many high-profile tragedies, for instance, the disintegration of an Air France Concorde supersonic airliner on takeoff from Paris in July 2000. I cannot urge too strongly that you make CFA an integral, regularly exercised element of the way you do decision management.

Numerous sources can provide you with specific techniques for performing good analyses, such as *Root Cause Analysis Handbook*.[2] But the spirit and way of thinking underlying CFA are far more important than the details of particular methods, which you should adapt to your own needs and tastes anyway. Thus it is useful to highlight the critical elements of the CFA perspective.

The first core idea of CFA as applied to decision management is that an analysis should be initiated whenever there is a sharp change in fortune for the company, the business equivalent of an airliner crash. The change *could* be positive, but people generally are more strongly compelled by negative changes—disasters. One or more decisions (or perhaps failures to decide) undoubtedly contributed to the focal incident. Suppose, for example, that the incident was a drastic increase in company losses, accompanied by sharp declines in share prices. The focal contributing decision was the selection of the new, ineffectual CEO, as noted in Figure 2.3, which is a cutout showing a small part of the "causal factor chart" you eventually assemble. Such a chart is simply a visual summary of a CFA.

The second core CFA idea to keep in mind is the aim of the analysis: the identification of correctable flaws in the company's normal decision processes. These flaws were betrayed by the specific failed decision at hand, but they are actually stable weaknesses and thus can be expected to cause repeated failures in the future. Concretely, your goal is to determine *addressable contributors* to the decision failure that occurred. An addressable contributor implicates a concrete feature of the decision process that if improved, would greatly reduce the odds of future disasters, and that can indeed be improved at a reasonable cost.

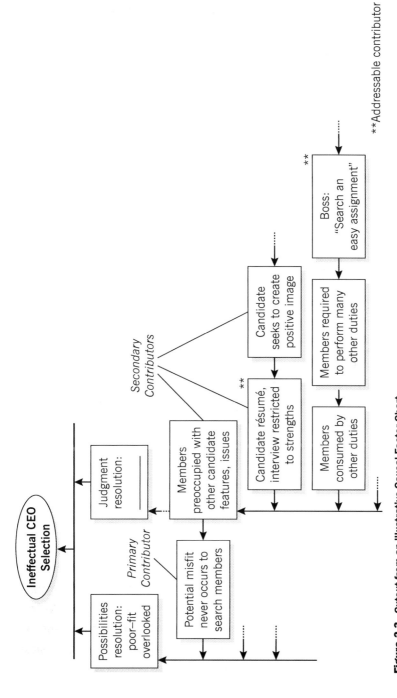

Figure 2.3. Cutout from an Illustrative Causal Factor Chart

The top tier of the chart in Figure 2.3 suggests the third core idea of CFA as applied to decision management: examine how the deciders resolved each of the ten cardinal decision issues. The cutout focuses on the part of the analysis concerning the possibilities issue. In this case, the resolution was poor in that the deciders failed to take into account a possibility that became only too evident once the CEO was on the scene—namely, that he was a poor fit with the company's culture. "Primary contributors" directly affect how an issue is resolved. Figure 2.3 focuses on one such primary contributor, the fact that potential lack of fit never even crossed the minds of the search committee members.

The chart also highlights the fourth and perhaps most important core idea in CFA—"cause pursuit." The decision managers performing the CFA must relentlessly ask, over and over and in sequence: "So why did that happen? . . . And why did *that* happen?" This yields chains of *secondary contributors*—contributors to contributors. For instance, in the chain at the bottom of Figure 2.3, you discover that search committee members failed to consider fit because they were preoccupied with other matters, which was in turn partly due to their having to attend to many other demanding duties. The members were required to perform those other duties because their boss erroneously believed that their search assignment was easier than it really was. Follow-up, confirmatory research, as required in CFA, showed that this manager routinely underestimates decision requirements. This contributor is addressable, as is the company's flawed interview procedure, which permits preoccupation with a candidate's strengths to the neglect of other considerations.

Your application of CFA, as well as cardinal issue checklists, will become more informed as you learn about the pitfalls associated with each issue and the countermeasures you can take to keep your company from falling into them. Based on these required foundations, it's time to move on with those issues, starting in the next chapter with the very first, the need issue.

CHAPTER SUMMARY

Taking advantage of sound decision management principles requires clear and precise thinking about the concepts involved. In particular, decisions are best understood as commitments to actions that are intended to produce satisfying states of affairs for the intended beneficiaries of those decisions. Besides the beneficiaries, typical parties to business decisions include the deciders, stakeholders, and decision managers.

The conception of an *effective decision* used in this book involves five criteria: aim, need, aggregated outcomes, rival options, and process costs. *Good decision processes* and *good deciders* are ones that tend to yield effective decisions. In practical situations, the goodness of decision processes (and deciders) is most easily assessed through examinations of how well those processes and deciders resolve the ten cardinal decision issues. Two highly useful tools that can help with these examinations (as well as with decision management generally) are cardinal issue checklists and causal factor analysis.

Questions for Consideration

1. Consider the four types of decisions distinguished in this chapter—choice, accept/reject, evaluation, and construction. Describe an illustration of each that you have seen in your company. In terms of the aim, need, aggregated outcomes, rival options, and process costs criteria, how effective were those decisions?

2. Some argue that the only people who can legitimately appraise the quality of a decision are the deciders. Others claim that it must be the beneficiaries. Still others say that people who had absolutely nothing to do with a decision are in the best position to assess its quality. In your view, ideally, who should be involved in assessing the quality of business decisions in your part of your company, and what should their specific roles be?

Deciding to Decide

The Need Issue

"They're gone, Geoff," says Byron Zahn, the vice president for marketing at Valley Power & Light Company.

"What do you mean, 'Gone'?" responds a worried Geoffrey Stone, Valley Power's CEO.

"As in, 'We're signing with Consolidated,'" replies Zahn. "I just spoke with Beth Finch over at Challenger, and she says they're dumping us for Consolidated when the contract is up. They say we're just too undependable."

This scenario is based on actual events described by an executive in the electric power industry. The company I'm calling Valley Power lost its long-term contract to supply electricity to one of its biggest industrial customers, Challenger

Manufacturing. The reason is that Valley's outages became so frequent that they created huge uncertainties and losses at Challenger. Challenger's managers were furious and said that they simply would not continue doing business that way, since with deregulation they now had options. So they chose to take their chances with Consolidated Energy, whose representatives claimed they could do better.*

The Valley Power incident illustrates what can happen when companies do a poor job of resolving Cardinal Decision Issue 1, the need issue. To appreciate precisely how, let me first lay out what is entailed in this issue generally. Then I will describe ways to ensure that your company resolves the need issue more successfully than did the managers at Valley Power.

■ The Need Issue

Chapter One introduced the need issue in these terms:

Why are we (not) deciding anything at all?

The need issue is thus about deciding to decide. To understand what this means, consider the metaphor illustrated in Figure 3.1. Imagine your company as an airplane in flight, cruising along the natural course of events. This is simply the path the company would follow if no decisions were made. The arrows heading toward that path represent future company-significant events (analogous to other airplanes, patches of clear sky, mountain ranges). Some of those events are negative—in the extreme, they are calamities (for instance, catastrophic generator break-

---

*This case, like all the other major illustrations in this book, is based on actual occurrences, although the details have been altered and fictionalized to disguise the identities of individuals and their companies.

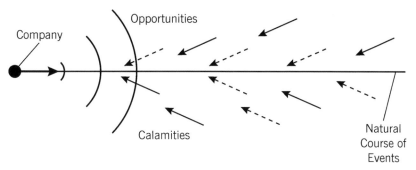

Figure 3.1. Monitoring the Natural Course of Events

downs at Valley Power). Others are positive opportunities that, if exploited, would advance the company's interests (for example, switching to the perspective of Valley's competitor, Consolidated Energy, the chance to pick off a prime customer). Each kind of event constitutes what I have termed a need. A company clearly needs to avoid every calamity. But the company needs to take advantage of the opportunities that come its way, too.

Actions taken to meet needs are the results of decision episodes. A *decision episode* is the story of a decision, with a beginning, a middle, and an ending. The beginning occurs when someone on the scene provides the spark by recognizing what is plausibly a significant company need to either avert a calamity or exploit an opportunity. ("We have a big issue here, and we have to decide what to do about it.") Meeting this apparent need constitutes the *aim* of the decision episode being initiated. The need issue is about how effectively the people in a company recognize when to initiate what sort of decision episode.

At Valley Power, Geoffrey Stone, Byron Zahn, and their colleagues missed a serious need. For years, Valley had enjoyed solid profits, high reliability, and low maintenance costs. Nothing in that benign scenario triggered any concerns about equipment. The sense that everything was basically fine continued even after Valley's equipment abruptly began deteriorating and creating costly maintenance problems. It took the Challenger Manufacturing incident to get management's attention. Only then did the managers conclude that they had to do something radical about reliability. In the terms used here, only then did they initiate a full-blown decision episode. But by that time, things had gotten so far out of hand that all of Valley's apparent options, such as retrofitting current equipment, building new plants, or purchasing power from the electric grid, were enormously expensive or risky. The leaders were so dismayed that they did nothing until independent consultants forecast that Valley's equipment would lose fully half of its capacity within five years. At that point, Valley's shell-shocked executives felt that they had no choice but to invest in major upgrades, at tremendous expense. Thus failure to recognize the need for a decision early on ultimately cost Valley Power dearly.

As a decision manager, your aim is to help assure that your company does not, like Valley Power, run afoul of the need issue. Actually, there are two different ways a company can do badly by the need issue, and therefore you face two different kinds of challenges:

- *Getting It Wrong, Version 1:* Everyone in the company fails to decide when there should have been a decision.
- *Getting It Wrong, Version 2:* Somebody in the company makes a decision when things would have been better had there been no decision effort at all.

Valley Power fell victim to Version 1: no one recognized the need to make a decision about maintenance problems, until it was too late. The more subtle and difficult case is Version 2, making a decision when it would have been better not to. I noted one way this can happen in Chapter Two: people in the company make decisions to meet what they perceive to be a significant need when there is actually no real need at all (recall

Greene/Jeffers deciding to form an alliance to protect itself against a nonexistent threat from a competitor). One important but easy-to-overlook reason to avoid this kind of mistake is that decision making is often quite expensive, for instance, entailing the high costs of searching out, investigating, and negotiating an agreement with a potential alliance partner.

The second version of getting it wrong can also occur when there is indeed a real company need, but the decision that is intended to meet that need is an ineffective one. In such cases, taking everything into account, the company would have been better off making no decision at all and continuing along the natural course of events depicted in Figure 3.1. This would have occurred at Valley Power if the company's executives had chosen to replace the company's worn out generators with third-rate equipment that made the company's situation even more precarious.

How do companies decide when to decide? Typically, companies pursue three different approaches to the need issue: obliviousness, demand response, and vigilance. At different times, you are likely to see all three approaches at play in your own company. The remainder of this chapter considers each of these approaches, with an emphasis on how you can help shape them to your company's benefit.

■ **Approach 1: Obliviousness**

The obliviousness approach to the need issue is actually a *non-approach*. In its purest form, a company would make no decisions at all, instead being blindsided and buffeted by whatever the world happens to throw its way. This would be analogous to the aircraft in Figure 3.1 simply flying along its preset path in blissful disregard for whatever might perchance lie on that path—be it fair weather, a lightning storm, or a mountain top. Thus, if profitable customers just happen to walk in the door asking for exactly what the company produces, the company will sell them its wares and prosper for it. But if a competitor comes along and entices away those customers, no one in the company would seek to craft measures to meet this challenge because no one would even notice it. The company would simply suffer the consequences.

In real life, there are no truly oblivious companies; if there were, they would rapidly be driven out of business. Yet many real companies—actually, the people who run them—sometimes do behave as if they had chosen a strategy of obliviousness. Perhaps because they were used to functioning in a noncompetitive, regulated environment, Valley Power's executives seemed frightfully out of touch with troubles brewing right inside their own facilities. In real-life cases of near-obliviousness, managers eventually do make decisions in response to needs pressing on their companies. The problem is that those decisions are often too little, too late. That is because two things happen over time, particularly in the case of impending calamities. First, as in the case of Valley's deteriorating equipment, unattended needs often grow stronger. Second, the options for meeting those needs (such as low-cost maintenance measures) grow weaker or disappear altogether.

Clearly, because for every business there are *always* emerging calamities and opportunities, your goal should be to steer your company away from obliviousness. But how? Start with the motivations: What are the attractions of obliviousness? Two stand out: costs and perceived value.

As I have noted, decision making involves costs. The most obvious strong suit of obliviousness is that it is cheap; nobody has to do or spend anything. In contrast, more active approaches to the need issue are undeniably costly. At Valley Power, for instance, actively monitoring the state of the company's equipment and the consequences of breakdowns might have involved such things as having high-priced power equipment consultants perform regular diagnoses of the machinery.

Sometimes the cost driver of obliviousness works indirectly. The people in the company are so preoccupied with other urgent functions—"running the business," they say—that they spend no time at all looking out for hazards and opportunities on the company's current path. Indeed, they might be so consumed by their other duties that the very idea of scanning the horizon never even crosses their minds. This is a cost issue because the company's leaders have crafted their budgets such that no one's paid workday has periods assigned to the task of looking ahead. The problem is especially endemic in new small businesses, more than half of which fail within the first five years. These companies are chronically undercapitalized. The result is that even the company heads must immerse themselves so deeply in operations that they have no time for the big picture.

When the cost motivator for obliviousness works directly, it is most typically framed in terms of affordability. Managers say things like, "We're fighting for survival. Unlike those other, big companies with whole strategy units, we just can't afford to waste money on folks sitting around pondering tomorrow. If we don't deal with the wolf at the door today, there won't *be* a tomorrow."

The second major driver of obliviousness is perceived value. Some managers genuinely believe that there is little to gain from looking ahead to spot potential calamities and opportunities. They note that lots of these hypothetical events prove to be false alarms, so that preparing for them is a waste of precious resources. They argue that it is smarter to maintain the company's agility, its ability to respond rapidly to calamities and opportunities at the point where there is no doubt they are real.

How do you combat the allure of obliviousness? One tack you can take is persuasion. For instance, you can make a case for seeking more financing than appears essential for simply running the business as it is currently envisioned. At least part of the "extra" financing would be earmarked for more active approaches to the need issue, such as those discussed later in the chapter. If you encounter the agility argument, you can concede the merits of agility while pointing out that even the most agile company cannot bring to heel problems that have raged out of hand for a long time.

Be prepared to meet people on their own ground, for example, by arguing that the risks of obliviousness are greater than its benefits. You will be especially convincing if you can provide your colleagues not only with logic but also with concrete examples, such as horror stories of companies similar to your own that have pursued obliviousness and suffered mightily for it.

■ Approach 2: Demand Response

"We got a request for a bid."
"We finished the Lancaster job, and naturally the crew wanted to know what's next."
"Their sales rep dropped by and made a pitch. Should we buy?"
"Jensen wants us to think about a merger."
"The shop steward says they aren't doing anything until we resolve this grievance."

Remarks like these are reflections of the demand response approach to the need issue: a decision to decide is prompted when someone places a demand on the company. Sometimes the decisions we make in response to demands are cursory dismissals; we stick with what we have after giving little or no serious consideration to the problems being posed. But in other instances, the demands spur us to initiate full-blown decision efforts.

Every business receives innumerable demands for decisions, and it can seldom simply ignore them. The issue here is not so much recognizing that some decision is called for, but rather dealing with demands appropriately and effectively.

Cost-effective filters are one key. A *filter* is a person (or group of persons) the company assigns to the task of screening certain kinds of requests. For a given request, the filter must ask and answer this question: "Can this request be dismissed out of hand (or can I grant it summarily), or does it demand further study?" If the dismissal question is answered yes, then, speaking for the company, the filter gracefully denies the request. If the answer is no, the filter forwards the request to other people for serious consideration, typically ones who have higher rank and whose time is more expensive (hence the cost savings of the approach). In effect, the filter is the person who initiates decision episodes, resolving the need issue for others.

The most familiar examples of filters are executives' staff assistants. While many managers recognize the usefulness of filters, seldom do they appreciate the need to substantively train filters, including staff assistants. Filters need to know enough about the business and its current strategy and conditions to make screens that are truly in the company's interests. Thus, when assistant Tom Barnes chooses to protect vice president Leah Meyer from having to devote her precious time to the Argus proposal, it is not because the proposal seems unpromising to him at a gut level. Instead, it is because the proposal clearly has little merit, given current company circumstances— which Meyer has taken great pains to make clear to him. Relying on filters who are ignorant about the business imposes a serious risk that executives who are theoretically being protected are actually being made oblivious.

The "3+ Rule" is another key to effective demand responses. The typical demand for a decision is more than that. It is a proposal—in effect, a request for an accept/reject decision, in the language of Chapter Two. The person making the demand (for instance, a sales representative) wants the company to pursue some particular course of action, one that typically is in that person's interests, which may or may not match the interests of the company. The 3+ Rule simply says that, if at all possible, when you receive an accept/reject demand, you should refuse to decide until you have identified at least two other alternatives that promise the same attractions that appealed to you in the original proposal. The comparisons will force your attention to important considerations that would otherwise escape your notice.

■ Approach 3: Vigilance

A major technology and manufacturing company that started as an auto parts supplier, which I will call UniFlex, maintains a small "futuring" group within its marketing research unit. The group's charge is to monitor the technological, economic, and social landscape ten years in the future and beyond. When the futuring group detects trends that might pose significant problems or opportunities for the company, it alerts UniFlex's leadership.

UniFlex's futuring group is a striking illustration of the vigilance approach to the need issue, which entails actively directing attention to anything and everything that potentially should prompt important decisions. Vigilance—*aggressive* vigilance—is an ideal that you, as a decision manager, can promote vigorously in your own company. It involves two distinct phases, monitoring and judging.

Phase 1: Monitoring

The first phase of vigilance, monitoring, involves making a spirited, proactive effort to scan the natural course for calamities and opportunities lying in wait. As suggested by the spreading arcs preceding the company in Figure 3.1, this is analogous to an airplane crew intensively scanning the vicinity of its flight path for other planes and hazards such as weather systems. Managers contemplating aggressive vigilance commonly ask three hard questions about monitoring that highlight important features of the approach.

Question 1: Who should monitor? Traditionally, companies expect and demand monitoring only from their top leaders. This is a mistake. Ideally, every employee should be encouraged to monitor and should be rewarded for doing a good job of it. That is because every employee, such as a customer service representative, is privy to company-significant facts known to nobody else.

For a long time, many companies have maintained robust employee suggestion programs, and the practice has grown in recent years.[1] Usually, these programs seek improvements in operations, such as refinements in assembly routines. But you can easily extend the idea (and specific techniques) to monitoring, requesting of everyone: "Talk to us about whatever you see or hear that seems significant to our business."

Question 2: Where should monitors look? A company obviously needs to monitor its competitors and customer base. But many of the developments in the world that will affect your company will come out of left field. Consider how delivery companies like United Parcel Service were radically affected by the transformation of the Internet from a network intended solely for military and scientific purposes into an electronic commerce medium. These companies had to decide on responses to the sharply increased demand for consumer deliveries and returns. Such decisions can be made most effectively when the needs they are intended to serve are anticipated far in advance. That is why numerous companies scan developments widely and far into the future. One major electronics company regularly recruits what its CEO describes as "bright, interesting people" in virtually any field to offer seminars to the company's managers. Invitees simply talk and answer questions about the ideas they are exploring, whether the connection to the company's core business is obvious or not. The managers then discuss among themselves what the connections might or might not eventually be.

Question 3: How often should monitors look? Some research suggests that in industries such as high technology, where things change rapidly, company leaders need virtually real-time data on the market, their competitors, and their own operations.[2] And those data must be reviewed at the same pace. Your own company's requirements might not be so stringent. Yet there is much to be said for normalizing the collection and discussion of current intelligence. Suppose that the executive committee for a unit in your company meets weekly. It would do well to reserve a sacred, untouchable slot on the agenda for intelligence review, where everyone is asked: "What have you learned that is happening outside and inside the unit, and what does it mean for us?" It might seem that this practice would slow things down. A surprising research discovery is that it actually *accelerates* decision making. One apparent reason is that everyone in the group is always up to speed on the facts needed to inform decisions; time-consuming briefings are unnecessary.

Phase 2: Judging

Assume that some people—call them *reporters*—are identifying lots of things that appear to be signals of calamities and opportunities for your company. Then there must be other people—call them *reviewers*—who are listening and making sense of those declarations. This is the judging phase of vigilance: distinguishing real from merely apparent calamities and opportunities, so that appropriate decision episodes are initiated—or not. To pursue the vigilance route, a company must plan, budget for, and train these reviewers to make accurate judgments.

Judgment is the province of Cardinal Decision Issue 6 and is addressed in its own right in a later chapter. The ideas there provide guidance on how to achieve judgment accuracy. One of those ideas, however, is so critical for vigilance that it is worth previewing here. There is a serious risk that aggressive monitoring will launch your company into the Chicken Little syndrome, scurrying off in all directions pursuing false calamities and opportunities. That is because people tend to draw (and then act on) strong conclusions on the basis of much less evidence than statistical principles say that they should.[3] Thus, when people see the slightest hint of a threat or opportunity, they cannot resist saying, "We must *do* something!"

This scientifically documented "variance-chasing" tendency is almost certainly a major reason that when real-time financial market data became widely available on the Internet, online traders sharply increased their trading activity while the quality of their trades, revealed in their losses, worsened.[4] To avoid a similar fate, your company's reviewers should establish a convention of refusing to conclude that apparent calamities and opportunities are real until they have verified them with more evidence than their intuitions suggest is actually necessary. This practice closely resembles one known to doctors as "watchful waiting" to see how a patient's suspicious symptoms develop.

Once the need for a decision is perceived—rightly or wrongly—the decision episode is ready to begin. But before anything can actually happen in that episode, the stage must be set, including settling on the players—that is, the deciders—and what resources are at their disposal. These essentials are the subject of the next chapter.

CHAPTER SUMMARY

Companies sometimes fail to decide when they should, but at other times they decide when they would be better off making no decisions at all. Managing the need issue is about preventing such mistakes.

Three main approaches to the need issue occur naturally: obliviousness, demand response, and vigilance. An effective decision management strategy steers the company away from the obliviousness approach, refines its accommodation of decision demands, and emphasizes aggressive vigilance. Table 3.1 summarizes the principal ways that you can implement such a strategy in your role as a decision manager.

Table 3.1. Managing the Need Issue

Key Need Issue Hazards and Challenges	Specific Recommendations
Failing to decide when should have decided	
■ Obliviousness	■ Alert to hazards; expose illusory appeal of low costs
■ Excessive faith in agility	■ Alert to risks
■ Uncritical dismissal of worthy proposals	■ Cost-effective, trained filters
■ Missed signals of calamities and opportunities	■ "Incentivized" routines for monitoring by all employees; signal analysis by trained judges
Deciding when should not have decided	
■ Uncritical acceptance of flawed proposals	■ The 3+ Rule
■ Misinterpreted signals, including "variance-chasing"	■ Signal analysis by trained judges; "watchful waiting"

Questions for Consideration

1. Describe the most serious instance you have observed firsthand in which a company suffered from mishandling the need issue. How would you explain what went wrong? Propose a specific decision management measure that a person holding a position like yours could take that would significantly reduce the odds of similar mishaps in that company in the future.

2. Imagine that your company succeeds in building enthusiastic employee participation in the task of monitoring plausible calamities and opportunities in the company's future. The vast majority of the employees' reports probably will prove to be false alarms. So you will need to put in place routines for telling individuals when their reports are indeed false alarms. What kinds of routines (including compensation schemes) would you use, given that you do not wish to dampen support for your program?

4

Determining the Means for Deciding

The Mode and Investment Issues

Paula Jackson, an executive at multibillion-dollar Superior Processing, tells the following story:

Historically, Superior has followed these signature authority rules:

Vice President	Over $4 million
Plant Manager	Over $1 million to $4 million
Unit Manager	Over $100,000 to $1 million
Department Manager	$0 to $100,000

So, for instance, a unit manager who wanted to make an expenditure between $100,000 and $1 million could just sign off on it without getting an approval from the boss.

A few months ago, Jim Forest was brought into Superior as the new vice president responsible for our division. One of the first things Jim did was unilaterally require his personal signature for any item that cost $100,000 or more. Wow, have things changed since then! Jim is now spending time on literally scores more decisions than his predecessor had to deal with, scrutinizing things at an incredible level of detail. It's nothing to see Jim in here before five in the morning and still at it at seven in the evening, weekends included. The plant and unit managers are baffled about what their roles are supposed to be these days. And lots of us are worried about the fact that since this has been going on, there's been virtually no discussion about the long-term and strategic issues facing the division.

Paula Jackson's observations vividly illustrate the focus of this chapter: determining the means for deciding. After a need in your company is acknowledged, somebody, or several somebodies, must get down to the nitty-gritty of making a decision that addresses that need. But who should those somebodies be, and how should they proceed? Further, what resources ought to be allocated to these efforts? What would be too much—or too little? These are the focal questions for the mode and investment issues.

■ The Mode Issue

This is how I articulate the mode issue, Cardinal Decision Issue 2:

> Who (or what) will make this decision, and
> how will they approach that task?

By *mode*, then, I mean determining, from among many possible options, how a particular decision or class of decisions will be made. At Superior Processing, Jim Forest resolved the mode issue for spending decisions differently from his predecessors, and the managers in his division obviously questioned the wisdom of his new scheme. What principles provide useful guidance to you, as a decision manager, when trying to think through such mode problems?

Choice Point 1: Authority

A helpful tool for thinking about the "how" of decisions is the mode tree depicted in Figure 4.1. The tree is organized according to the critical choices decision managers make—whether they realize it or not—when they settle on the modes used in making various kinds of decisions.

The top level of the mode tree, Choice Point 1, concerns decision authority: who (or what, as I will explain later) is commonly acknowledged as responsible for a particular class of decision. Sometimes such authority is formally codified, for instance, in laws governing the responsibilities of corporations' boards of directors, in a firm's by-laws, or in a division's written procedures. More often, though, authority conventions are informal, having simply evolved over the years. ("Gee, beats me. We've *always* had Geraldine make work assignments.")

You will rarely hear people talking about decision authority questions in an ordinary business day. Authority conventions are so much a part of the natural order of things in any company that no one thinks much about them. But you *will* see authority questions receive great attention in two circumstances: when, for whatever reason, existing conventions are changed (as when Jim Forest changed the rules at Superior Processing) and when a new business structure is created (as in a major reorganization or when a new entity is formed because of a merger, a joint venture, or a decision to spin off a new company). At such times, the need to determine who will decide what kinds of issues is obvious.

As a decision manager, you can direct attention to authority conventions not only in cases of obvious need but when no one is giving them much thought. Problems concerning decision

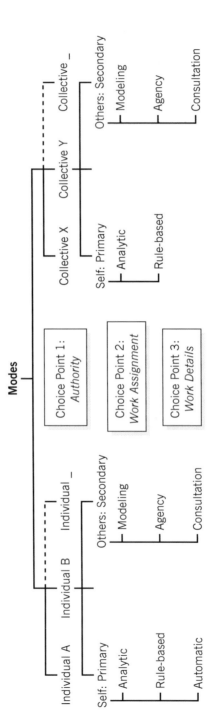

Figure 4.1. The Mode Tree

authority speak most directly to the "shaping decision customs" element of your decision management portfolio. If, like Jim Forest, you are fully in charge of some unit in your company, you can probably set authority conventions as you wish. More generally, though, conventions are established and changed through negotiations among lots of people, and you will influence those conventions through your ability to persuade others.

What principles can you turn to as you strive to establish good authority conventions? Imagine that you are part of a team assigned to lead a new spinoff and this question comes up: "Where should we put decisions about whether to develop particular products, solely in the hands of the product development VP or in the marketing committee's bailiwick?" As you deliberate, the following questions should be cycling through your head like a mantra: If we assigned authority that way, how effective would the resulting decisions be? That is, typically, how well would the various cardinal decision issues be resolved?

One Decider or More?
Concretely, as suggested by Figure 4.1, the first specific question to resolve is whether to assign authority to an individual or to a collective, for instance, a committee or a series of officials who must each sign off on a particular action. What you advocate in any particular instance should rest on the gains and losses of collective versus individual decision making with respect to the cardinal decision issues. These gains and losses are summarized in Table 4.1.

First, the gains:

- *Gain 1: Collective coverage.* To a point, we all accept the maxim, "Two (or more) heads are better than one." Research has shown, though, that we *under*appreciate how *much* better. In one study, for example, people were asked to bring to mind potential solutions to a parking crisis and then to estimate how many viable options they had overlooked, including options that other

Table 4.1. **Common Gains and Losses from
Decision Making by Collectives Rather Than Individuals**

Gains	Losses
G1: Collective coverage	L1: Compensation costs
G2: Division of labor and specialization	L2: Coordination costs
G3: Value sensitivity	L3: Shared information effect
G4: Acceptance	L4: Evasion of responsibility
G5: Development	L5: Amplification of bad norms

people might have brought to mind.[1] The participants in the study grossly underestimated what they had missed.

The diagrams in Figure 4.2 illustrate what this means. Each oval represents decision-relevant considerations one individual brings to mind. As suggested in the top panel, we rightly suspect that several people collectively think of more considerations than any one of them. But in reality, as represented in the bottom panel, the amount of overlap in what they envision is less than we generally imagine. Put more positively, the "collective coverage" of groups is better than we expect. That is because individuals differ more than we realize in terms of how they see the world and the problems confronting them.

Groups therefore have much greater potential than any single individual for bringing to mind the full panoply of factors that bear on any decision. Moreover, the scope of those considerations is broader than we assume. This point has direct implications for several cardinal decision issues, but especially those concerning options and possibilities. (What are the different actions we could take to deal with this problem, and what could potentially happen if we did those things?)

- *Gain 2: Division of labor and specialization.* Any one person can do only so much work and can know only some of the things required for an effective decision. Through division of labor and specialization, groups provide a way to deal with this

A. What People Expect

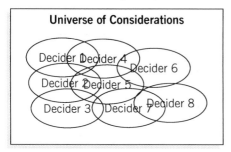

B. Reality

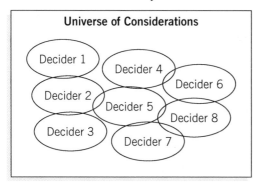

Figure 4.2. Schematic Representation of Collective Coverage

reality. This advantage is especially important for the kinds of complex problems, so common in business today, that demand the expertise of numerous specialists (for instance, lawyers, engineers, and physicians). This has particular significance for the judgment issue. (Which of the things they care about actually would happen if we took that action?)

■ *Gain 3: Value sensitivity.* Many decision problems require us to anticipate how people will feel about something, for example, a new service or a change in company compensation policies. In such cases the value and acceptability issues take center stage. (Will they hate this policy—to the point where they give us a lot of grief?) Once again, people differ more than we suspect—in this case, in their values or tastes. As with collective coverage, a group necessarily has a better chance than any one individual of being in touch with the variety of tastes that often spell the difference between a decision that succeeds and one that fails. Of course, the more diverse the group in relevant respects, the greater the advantage.

- *Gain 4: Acceptance.* Collective decisions have immediate advantages with respect to the acceptability issue (How can we get them to agree to this decision and this decision procedure?) and, thereby, the implementation issue (How can we get it done?), since people who accept a decision rarely try to sabotage its enactment. So, for instance, people more readily accept a rejection from a collective than an individual. Part of the reason is that we tend to believe that two (or more) heads are indeed better than one. If John Wilson rejects your proposal, you can easily say, "Wilson is being his usual biased, ill-informed self." It is harder to make the same judgment when the rejection comes from a nine-person committee, especially if the committee includes several people you perceive as being just like yourself.

- *Gain 5: Development.* A final advantage of collectives is that they help develop decision-making talent. Thus, even though you are perfectly capable of making budget allocation decisions yourself, it is wise to have junior members of your staff involved in the process so that they can learn to make those decisions, too.

Now, the losses often associated with deciding collectively:

- *Loss 1: Compensation costs.* Collective decision making is obviously more expensive; you must pay several people instead of just one. This clearly bears on the investment issue. (How much should we spend making this decision?)

- *Loss 2: Coordination costs.* You can surely remember countless meetings where you moaned to yourself, "I could have done this in fifteen minutes all by myself." Although getting people to work together productively is usually not impossibly difficult, it does require effort and time—and often lots of both. These coordination costs are real in and of themselves, and they often translate more or less directly into financial costs for the company as well.

- *Loss 3: Shared information effect.* You often want several particular people to make a complex decision because each of them knows things the others do not; they can all bring different things to the table. Unfortunately, as a substantial line of research has shown, there is an excellent chance that those different things will never actually reach the table. Instead of each person offering specialized knowledge, the group will tend to talk about things they all know.[2] Hence the term "shared information effect." Its consequences are most clearly apparent for judgment accuracy, the judgment issue. In principle, for instance, having a group of expert specialists work as a team should yield exceptionally accurate forecasts of various outcomes of a merger. But their actual accuracy will probably fall short because that expertise is not fully exploited. One way you can reduce the odds of the effect occurring is to keep deliberations going beyond the first point where people are inclined to remark, "So, since we are all in agreement—" Say things like, "I'm not so sure, Chuck. Speaking as a pricing specialist, what do *you* think, Sharon?"

- *Loss 4: Evasion of responsibility.* You have surely experienced the truth of the expression, "If it's everybody's job, then it's nobody's job. It won't get done." Such evasion of responsibility is a significant hazard of collective decision making. Numerous studies have shown that every person in a group feels less responsible for what the group achieves—or does *not* achieve—than the same person would feel if solely responsible. This reduced commitment bodes ill for decision quality in almost every respect.

- *Loss 5: Amplification of bad norms.* Suppose that all the members of a group (or even most of them) adhere to some particular norm, say, avoiding risk. Then, when the group works in concert, that norm emerges in spades. If the norm is supportive of effective decisions, terrific. But if the norm is problematic, its amplification in the group can spell real trouble for decision quality. Consider risk taking.[3] Picture a company that has a norm for risk aversion, and imagine that several people in the company are charged with making certain investment decisions. Those decisions will be significantly more conservative than if any of the group's members were deciding alone, and this conservatism might well be contrary to the company's interests.

So, in a specific case, should you advocate that authority for a particular class of decisions be assigned to a group or to the person occupying one particular position? To answer that question, you need to assess the status of each of the forces sketched in Table 4.1 and determine whether, in that instance, their balance favors or opposes collective deliberation. The answer varies from one decision problem to the next. For example, since decisions about how to classify particular expenses require accounting expertise and are relatively uncontroversial, it makes sense to assign them to one person. But decisions about large-scale layoffs demand diverse insights and are fraught with acceptability hazards, thereby warranting collective decision making.

Resistance. You need not worry inordinately about resistance from other people when authority for some class of decision is being established for the first time, as in a new spinoff. But you should worry a lot when you wish to change authority rules already in place. Witness, for instance, the resentment created by Jim Forest when he changed expenditure sign-off rules at Superior Processing. Part of the resistance created by changes comes from incumbents whose authority is diminished and who feel as if they have just been demoted. But you will almost surely get resistance from others who have accommodated themselves to what was in place before, and who dread the uncertainty and the work of accommodating themselves to the new rules. (The "Better the devil you know" reaction.) Besides, they will probably have come to consider the current rules sensible. Those rules will have also benefited from the *mere exposure effect:* people tend to become more positive about virtually anything to which they have been exposed repeatedly.

All this means that you should think twice before changing decision authority assignments. Ask yourself: "Given all the trouble this will cause, is it really worth our while making this change? Will the decisions be so much more effective that it's worth the hassle?" If the answer is yes, then make the change carefully, with due consideration to the ideas in Chapter Eight, which discusses the acceptability issue in detail. A couple of points from that chapter are worth a preview here. The first is that, unlike Jim Forest at Superior Processing, you should give a rationale for the change; people hate silent imperiousness. The second is that you should be prepared to negotiate the change with the people it affects, perhaps offering compensation for the troubles imposed on them.

Culture. Often companies find themselves in a situation where decision authority conventions must be established for people from a different culture. By *culture,* I mean, first, "company culture," a consideration in mergers, acquisitions, joint ventures, and the like. Since at least some of the people in the new entity are being asked to change their customs, the remarks about smoothing the way for change apply.

A second important sense of *culture* refers to the collected customs or ways of doing things shared by people in a particular part of the world, for instance, Japan as contrasted with France. Among such customs are decision authority conventions. If you wish (or need) to learn more about such cultural differences, numerous sources are available.[4] But suppose that your company is about to embark on a joint enterprise with a company from another country or one where many of the employees come from a different culture. A couple of basic pieces of advice would be useful to keep in mind. First, expect that the people from the other culture might very well be accustomed to, and prefer, conventions different from those you favor (even though they might be too polite or fearful to tell you openly). Second, carefully observe (and ask about) what their preferred customs actually are, and then negotiate the conventions to be followed.

Which Individuals?

As shown in Figure 4.1, once you have resolved the question of assigning decision authority to a collective or to an individual, the next question is, *which* individual or collective should get the assignment? I'll take up the case of individuals first.

Suppose your company has chosen to assign some class of decisions to a particular position. How should the company choose which person should fill the position? You will, of course, consider candidates in light of all the duties of the position. But when evaluating candidates in terms of their ability to make a certain class of decisions, the question to ask is this: "Who has the best track record making decisions like these?" If such records do not exist, the next best question is, "How *likely* is it that the candidate will make those decisions well?" These judgments, in turn, should be driven by informed opinions about the candidates' chances of successfully addressing every cardinal decision issue. Among other things, this point should suggest the kinds of inquiries you make about the candidates, including questions to ask when you interview them.

Which Leaders and Members?

Now suppose that the company has concluded that a group, say, a committee, should make a certain type of decision. What kinds of people should be picked to lead and constitute the group?

In choosing the leader, it is not critical to pick someone especially good at making the pertinent decisions, although you should certainly respect competence in this area. What is most important is that the leader should have good group decision management skills. More specifically, the leader should understand that an effective decision rests on adequately addressing all the cardinal decision issues and be skilled at making certain that all those issues are covered well by the group for every decision.

As with the leader, it is not essential that the other members of the group be especially good personal decision makers. Instead, adopt a portfolio or team perspective when assembling the group. Just like an athletic team, a successful business team includes people who *collectively* possess all the knowledge and skills required for the task at hand. In the case of a decision team, that means the group collectively has everything it needs to assure that every cardinal decision issue is adequately resolved for the decisions in question.

Choice Point 2: Work Assignment

Decision *authority* is one thing; decision *work*—actually thinking a decision problem through—is another. The party authorized to make a decision has two alternatives, as suggested at Choice Point 2 in Figure 4.1: either figure the problem out alone or else redirect some or all of that responsibility elsewhere. The former option involves *primary modes* of deciding, the latter *secondary modes*.

Imagine, for example, that your customer service manager, Clark Munger, has been authorized to handle complaints about your products. Recently, he has received a sudden flood of complaints about the XS75, a key item in your company's product line. Munger could, per his prerogative, decide completely on his own what to do about the problem (via one of the primary modes of deciding to be discussed shortly) or he could involve other people or resources (via a secondary mode). What should he do? More generally, as a decision manager, how can you help make sure that authorized deciders make effective decision work assignments?

An initial observation: More often than not, especially for decision problems that are out of the ordinary, authorized deciders take a hybrid approach to decision work assignments. That is, they break the problem into parts and assign the work for some aspects of the problem to others while retaining some aspects for themselves.

The fundamental question the authorized decider needs to ask and answer is this: "All things considered, including costs, who can figure things out better, myself or somebody else, and if the latter, who?" (Note that the "somebody else" actually could be a *something* else, such as an expert system or other computer program.) To assure that this question is answered effectively, you should promote two customs among authorized deciders in your company: self-assessment and awareness of alternative means.

Work Assignment Custom 1: Self-Assessment. Part of the custom of self-assessment is the habit of simply asking oneself, "Is it possible that I'm not the best person for doing this?" We are not naturally inclined to ask this question, partly because it is threatening to our cherished positions as authorized deciders. Thus, you will have to get buy-in from all involved that it is not just OK but a *positive responsibility* for authorized deciders to ask this question and to answer yes when that is in fact the right answer. So, for example, Clark Munger should not have to worry that his competence will be questioned if he brings the unprecedented spate of complaints about the XS75 to the attention of his boss.

Of course, self-assessment is only useful insofar as it is accurate (a judgment issue of the kind discussed in Chapter Six). There is reason to worry on this score. Numerous studies indicate that you should expect gross overconfidence. More often than we should, we say, "I'm probably better at this than most folks, and certainly any dumb machine. So I'll do it myself." This is not solely or even primarily an inflated ego talking. Great confidence is understandable (even if misplaced) given that we have encountered little direct evidence that we cannot handle a particular task well. So we give ourselves the benefit of the doubt. For instance, Clark Munger has never seen anything like the rash of XS75 complaints. Yet he has done fine with other complaint situations, so why should he doubt himself on the XS75? The moral is that companies need to train their deciders to be on guard against the natural tendency to overestimate their own competence, particularly when it comes to novel decision situations.

Work Assignment Custom 2: Awareness of Alternative Means. To assign decision work to a person or device better able to perform the task, the decider must know both who or what those other people and devices are and how proficient they are, particularly relative to the decider. We can easily be clueless about both. A good illustration is a case described to me by a consulting engineer at a company I will call EnviroSim. The incident involved erosion simulations needed for a client; the company's local office could not produce acceptable simulations with the programs it had on hand. The division manager had been away from engineering school for quite some time and had not kept current with simulation developments outside his immediate area. He was therefore unaware of off-the-shelf programs that offered exactly what he needed. The situation was compounded by the manager's fear of bothering his superiors with his doubts about the adequacy of the programs on hand. The ultimate result was disastrous service to the client that nearly destroyed the division's reputation and, indeed, that of EnviroSim. The odds of such incidents are greatly reduced when deciders keep abreast of decision tools and experts in their area and routinely have their plans for major, unusual decisions scrutinized by peers—as simple as asking, "Hey, what do you think?"

Choice Point 3: Work Details

The third choice point in Figure 4.1 is about how the details of
the decision work will actually be carried out. This choice point
differs from the first two in that the detail mode that winds up
being used is sometimes not deliberately chosen in the sense that
we normally think of choice. The possible modes differ according to whether the authorized decider does the work—primary
modes—or has shifted it elsewhere—secondary modes.

Primary Detail Modes
There are three primary detail modes: analytic, rule-based, and
automatic. I will first define each of these modes and then consider the decision management challenges they present.

▪ *Analytic mode:* Think back to the last committee meeting
you attended where a significant, out-of-the-ordinary decision
was made, for instance, about abandoning a major service your
company had provided to customers for years. Undoubtedly,
what happened seemed messy, difficult, and even painful. There
were no holds barred; the rule seemed to be "no rules, anything
goes." People fought tooth and nail, offering every argument
imaginable in their efforts to figure out what to do and to persuade others that they had indeed figured out what to do. That
was analytic decision making:

Analytic decision making is the unconstrained,
purposeful, and effortful reasoning through to a conclusion
about what action makes sense to pursue in a given situation.

An important aside: Analytic decision making—whether
by a group or just one person—generally looks chaotic, but those
impressions are deceptive. A big part of your job as a decision
manager, particularly in your role as a facilitator of group deliberations, is ensuring that effective decisions emerge from the

seeming disorder. A key to doing that is recognizing how people's actions amount to their attempts to resolve particular cardinal decision issues and then helping them reach good resolutions. For instance, the following kinds of heated remarks are not unusual: "Elaine, you can't be serious! That's not how things work in this market. This is how they work . . . " Whereupon the speaker proceeds to draw conclusions such as: "Now this is the kind of thing that can happen . . . " (implicating the possibilities issue) or, more strongly, "If we do what you're suggesting, Elaine, I can guarantee you that in six months . . . " (pursuing the judgment issue). By recognizing which decision issue is at stake, you can apply what you learn in this book to help the deciders resolve that issue successfully.

- *Rule-based mode:* A "decision rule" has the following form:

> If Condition C holds, then pursue Option A.

A simple example is a retail stocking rule: "Reorder when only 5 units remain." In many decision rules, "Condition C" consists of several constituent conditions. An example is a set of rules for loan approvals, where the condition for getting an applicant to the second stage of the process consists of several requirements like "Has worked in the area for six months or more," "Has monthly income above $2000," and so on. Thus we have rule-based decision making:

> Rule-based decision making is the deliberate
> attempt to match the circumstances of a given
> situation to the precondition of a decision rule and
> then pursue the action prescribed by that rule.

- *Automatic mode:* Picture clerk George Blair working in one of your company's stores. An irate customer suddenly becomes abusive to Blair, calling him obscene names and gesturing wildly. Without thinking, Blair immediately responds in kind, escalating a nasty scene witnessed in horror by several other customers. What they observed was the manifestation of automatic decision making:

> Automatic decision making is the effortless
> and uncontrollable evocation of an action sequence.

Such sequences can be denoted compactly like so: $S: St \rightarrow A$, where St represents a state of affairs which, if perceived (perhaps nonconsciously) by the person in question, automatically and mindlessly triggers action A. When George Blair perceived himself as under attack, his retaliation simply popped out, seemingly of its own accord. ("I'm really sorry," he told his boss later, "but it just *happened!*") By its nature, automatic decision making is peculiar to individual deciders, which is why it does not appear under the collective decision branch in the mode tree in Figure 4.1.

Why are these distinctions between primary detail modes important? Because deciders sometimes apply one primary mode when it would have been better to apply another. Your job as a decision manager is to help deciders prevent that from happening. One key to doing that is understanding exactly what inappropriate application of these modes means. Another is understanding how and why misapplication occurs. Two special cases highlight the key ideas: problematic rule-based decision making and problematic automatic decision making.

- *Problematic rule-based decision making:* From its inception, the middle market loan officers at what I will call Reliance Bank pretty much had a free hand in deciding on loans. Each officer approached the task analytically. In due course, however, Reliance's managers became distressed about several aspects of the loan officers' decision making:

- *Performance:* Although some officers' loans performed exceptionally well, defaults on others hurt the bank badly.

- *Consistency:* As suggested by the observation on perform-ance, there was worrisome inconsistency in the officers' decisions.
- *Cost:* At least some officers were slow in making loan deci-sions, which translated into unacceptable costs.

These concerns motivated a decision to move from analytic to rule-based decision making. Pertaining to performance, Re-liance's managers reasoned: "Why not figure out the best rule for deciding on these loans and just have everybody apply that rule?" Pertaining to consistency, they argued: "If everyone is fol-lowing the same rule, our inconsistency problem will have solved itself." About costs, they submitted: "Why should every loan officer reinvent the wheel for every application? With a sound rule, they should be able to work a lot faster—and more cheaply." These are all among the most common justifications for attempting rule-based decision making.

So what could go wrong? What *did* go wrong, and why? The major problems included these:

- *Rule performance:* The loans made via the new rules did not, on average, outperform loans vetted according to the old system.
- *Rule fit:* Loan officers complained that there were often as-pects of applicants' situations that had implications for the wisdom of granting loans but were simply not covered in the rules.
- *Resistance:* Although they did acknowledge that the rules en-abled them to explain exactly why a loan was granted or de-nied, on the whole, the loan officers hated following the rules for several reasons: deciding "by the book" was rigid and unnatural; it forced them to ignore things they felt were pertinent; and it was demeaning, effectively reducing them to clerks.

□

Each of these problems is among those often observed when rule-based decision making goes bad. This is not to say that you should discourage rule-based decision making altogether: to do so would be foolish even if it were possible. If you look carefully, you will recognize perhaps scores of decision rules used routinely in any company. Because of their efficiencies, they are indispensable. The main lesson of experiences like the one at Reliance is that, in every specific instance, managers need to carefully judge the likelihood of hazards, including rule weakness, lack of fit, and resistance. In some cases, there might be no available rule that demonstrably outperforms the analytic decision practices already in place. In other situations, there is the potential to manage the risks. For instance, Reliance might have reduced its loan officers' resistance by involving them in the process improvement effort from Day 1, including the task of making rule use enjoyable rather than degrading (and perhaps devising more complex or flexible rules as a result of the loan officers' input).

- *Problematic automatic decision making:* Concerns about automatic decision making in business are mainly (though not exclusively) confined to decisions in operational contexts, where things happen fast. Some examples: customer interactions, as in the George Blair incident; trading on the floor of a commodities market; controlling production equipment in an assembly or power plant, where catastrophic accidents can occur at any moment. In situations like these, speed is at a premium; we want and need the instantaneous action that automaticity provides. The problematic cases are the ones in which those instantaneous actions are the wrong ones.

You can help your company reduce the odds of problematic automatic decisions by understanding their origins and dynamics. Frequently, automatic decision making results from this developmental sequence:

Analytic → Rule-Based → Automatic

To illustrate this sequence, recall learning to drive. The first time you had to decide when and how to merge into an expressway full of cars whizzing by at eighty miles per hour, the process was painfully analytic. Your driving instructor—if you had one— suggested some decision rules that you gradually memorized, or else you developed your own rules. Eventually, those rules became automatized to the point where now you often find yourself in the middle of the traffic flow and (scarily) cannot even remember how you got there.

One hazard of this developmental sequence is that there is no guarantee that the rules that become automatized are good ones. With sufficient repetitions, even bad rules inevitably automatize. Hence bad drivers, bad floor traders, and bad process operators. And hence one important prescription for trainers: be vigilant observing each trainee's repeated actions from the very beginning of training. Whatever the trainee does over and over— whether functional or dysfunctional—will solidify.

Whereas the developmental sequence summarizes how repeated decisions tend toward automaticity, the following episodic sequence describes how modes emerge in a specific decision episode:

If a triggering state is recognized, experience: Automatic →
    If no triggering state is recognized, try: Rule-based →
    If no rule applies, resort to: Analytic

That is, if the decider happens to perceive the triggering state for an automatized action sequence, the action prescribed by that sequence *will happen,* without any conscious intent on the part of the decider (recall George Blair's retaliation against his customer). Other modes of deciding will occur only if automatic decision making *cannot* occur (because no triggering state is recognized). For reasons of ease, deciders will then usually try to find an applicable decision rule. Only as a last resort will they turn to analytic decision making.

This episodic sequence is exceptionally important. Suppose that an employee makes a certain type of decision badly as a result of a dysfunctional automatized action sequence. The manager's natural inclination is to reason with the employee, to urge greater care and effort. (*"Think* and do the right thing!") This tack might make sense if the behavior were driven by analytic decisions, but it is useless when the action rests on automatic decisions, which simply pop out when the right conditions are present. Consider what some smoking cessation trainers do when they discover that a client habitually and unconsciously reaches into his shirt pocket, fetches cigarettes, and lights up. As an early step in the training program, they interrupt such automatized action sequences by having clients move their cigarettes from the customary location to another one. This prevents the action sequence from completing itself and so forces the decision to light up to be an analytic one, one that has a better chance of being, "Maybe not this time." As a decision manager, you can adapt the logic of this approach to repairing the problematic automatic decision making you observe.

Secondary Detail Modes
As depicted in Figure 4.1, when the authorized decider chooses to assign working through the details of a decision problem to others, the decider has three options: the modeling, agency, and consultation modes.

- *Modeling mode:* In this mode, the decider involves others in the sense of reaching the decision by simply imitating the action of a respected model. Benchmarking is a good illustration, for example, adopting the same supply chain software as the industry leader *because* the industry leader is using it.

- *Agency mode:* Here, an *agent* is a party the authorized decider commissions to make the decision in question, start to finish. All delegations of decision-making authority, as when you turn over the hiring of clerical staff to your second-in-command, are instances of the agency mode. We normally think of decision agents as being people, but they do not have to be. Computerized trading programs that buy and sell securities when particular price targets are hit are good illustrations of nonhuman agents.

- *Consultation mode:* In the present context, a *consultant* is one who offers one or more recommendations, either for the ultimate action the authorized decider might pursue or, more modestly, for some element that is required in the decision process. Or the consultant could be more neutral, simply providing decision-relevant information. This mode is distinct from the agency mode in that the authorized decider retains the task of making the final decision. Your company's executive officers are usefully viewed as consultants for the board of directors; they routinely provide many of the options and virtually all of the requisite facts used to inform the board's decisions. Reviewers, such as the authors of the product rankings that are so popular these days (including business school rankings), are consultants in this sense, too. On the home front, when your washer breaks down and you look up what *Consumer Reports* has to say about possible replacements, you have, in effect, hired the magazine's writers as your consultants.

Picture your company using one of the secondary detail modes and getting burned for it. How and why might that happen, and what can you do to help prevent recurrences?

First I need to specify what *getting burned* means: it means that more effective decisions would have been made by other means. Obvious as this point seems, companies seldom bother to ask after the fact whether they did indeed get burned. Hence, they are readily burned again. For present purposes, what considerations come into play when evaluating how a company might get burned in its choice of secondary detail modes?

- *Costs:* One particular dimension of decision effectiveness warrants special attention in this context—costs. For example, the modeling mode is essentially free, whereas agents and consultants can be costly indeed, and a company can easily pay too much. Principles to guide thinking about how much is too much are discussed later in this chapter in connection with the investment issue.

■ *The wrong people:* The most serious hazard of secondary detail modes is that a company chooses to rely on the wrong people. For example, one might choose to imitate a poor model. One side of this problem is that the action pursued by the model might not actually be serving the model's interests as assumed. Thus you select your industry leader's supply chain software because you attribute at least some of the leader's success to that software. But that attribution could be a mistake; indeed, the leader might even be dissatisfied with its choice. The general principle is that the adequacy of a model's chosen action needs to be documented. Another side of the problem of picking the wrong model is that what is good for the model might not be good for your company. Thus the leader's supply chain software might work poorly in combination with the suite of programs used at your company, which happen to be markedly different from those of the leader. The moral? Before embracing a model's choice, the decider needs to make sure that the model's action is applicable to the decider's own circumstances.

Similarly, it is easy to pick the wrong agent or consultant. One reason is that agents and consultants naturally present themselves in the best light. Accordingly, they emphasize features they have learned impress clients (or bosses) and deflect attention from everything else. The second reason interacts with the first: deciders often fail to demand the things they need to know in order to properly appraise a prospective agent or consultant. Etch this "Behavior Prediction Law" into your consciousness:

The best predictor of future behavior is past behavior.

So if a company wants to anticipate how well a consultant might perform for its project, it should require and carefully appraise records of the consultant's performance on similar projects in the past. Studies have indicated that (perhaps partly because of politeness) people are disinclined to make such demands naturally.[5] Instead, we are strongly swayed by things like how confident prospective consultants appear and their ability to convincingly articulate explanations, things that can be easily faked.

- *Incentive misalignment:* The final hazard concerns an agent or consultant's motives. Your company's deciders must always ask: "They recommended X but denigrated Y. If we pursued X, would the consultant be better off?" If the answer is yes, there is the potential of incentive misalignment: your consultant, consciously or otherwise, might be seeking to serve personal interests at the expense of your own. This happens more often than deciders realize.

■ The Investment Issue

Engineer Hank Collins told me, "We recently had to decide which of three different kinds of safety testing equipment we should install in our lab at Precision Technologies. We eventually spent about $50,000 making that decision." Was $50,000 excessive, insufficient, or about right? This question illustrates the investment issue, Cardinal Decision Issue 3:

> What kinds and amounts of resources will be invested
> in the process of making this decision?

Resolving this issue poorly bears on the effectiveness of decisions in two ways. If too much is spent, the effect is direct: the resulting decision is, by definition, deficient in terms of the process costs criterion. If spending is too little, there will be indirect effects: the deciders will be unable to ensure success with respect to all the other criteria of decision effectiveness, such as achieving the aims of the decision.

Resource Classes

Two classes of resources matter. The first are *material* resources, that is, money and things that translate more or less directly into money. One such resource is deciders' time. Another is represented by effort or energy (as when you complain after thinking really hard on a decision problem, "I'm just wiped out").

The second class of resources is *emotional*—deciders' capacity for withstanding agitation and distress. It is implicated in remarks like the following:

"This is really painful!"
"I simply can't stand this uncertainty, this tension."
"We can't agree, and it's tearing our office apart."

In many situations, the emotional resources consumed by decision making are at least as important as the material resources. Moreover, they are often inescapable. For instance, risk is inherent in most high-stakes decision problems, as acknowledged in admissions of fears like these:

"Suppose I get it wrong? That would make the company lose *millions!*"
"I would be destroying people's jobs—my friends' jobs."
"I would look really stupid."
"I could get fired."

Research has amply demonstrated that sustained exposure to the kind of distress people experience in the presence of such risks can literally kill.[6] Thus your ability to help your company work through the investment issue with respect to costs other than material ones has palpable significance.

Guiding Principles

Unfortunately, there are no formulas that can tell you exactly how much your company should spend making a given decision. Most business decision situations are far too complicated and messy for that. There are, however, several sound principles that provide useful guidance in thinking about how much to invest in the process of making particular decisions.

Principle 1: Limits
Do not invest more than the potential gain.

In other words, the possible benefits of a decision must, at minimum, cover the costs of making that decision. You would immediately see the foolishness of a football fan who spends $10 on a Las Vegas tip sheet for advice on how to structure a $5 bet with his buddy. Yet you can undoubtedly recall deciders wasting valuable time (and hence money) agonizing over trivial decisions whose stakes simply did not warrant so large an investment.

Managers often violate the limits principle because of a kind of obliviousness, as they admit, "Frankly, we didn't even *think* about how much we were spending on that decision." It is therefore wise to promote among deciders the rare mindfulness represented here: "We just asked Caldwell to drop everything else he's doing and compile a huge report for us. What are the odds that that report will make our decision so much better that Caldwell's troubles will prove justified?" Other violations of the limits principle rest on the fact that, as research has shown, some people are simply indecisive; decision making upsets them and thus they agonize over it. Whenever feasible, indecisive staff members should not be forced to make time-sensitive company decisions.

Principle 2: Reducible Decision Risk
Expend decision resources in relation to the decision risk that is re-
ducible by that expenditure.

The expression *decision risk* refers to the chance that making a decision in a particular fashion will result in an awful decision, that is, one that is exceptionally ineffective. Sometimes
alternative ways of making the decision will reduce the decision risk, and sometimes not. By Principle 2, you would invest
decision-making resources only in the former case.

As a contrived yet instructive example, imagine two possible investment opportunities. In Situation A, you have the opportunity to invest $5000 in a scheme whose returns depend on
hog belly prices three years from now. In Situation B, your opportunity is to invest $5000 in the new restaurant being opened
by your brother-in-law. There is essentially nothing useful that
anyone can tell you about hog belly prices three years hence, so
you would be foolish to pay for anything a consultant might tell
you. In contrast, it would make perfect sense to pay a restaurant expert to appraise the prospects for the new restaurant.
And you should be willing to pay more according to the degree
to which that expert's advice can reduce your risk of losing all
your money.

Principle 3: Decision Planning and Budgeting
Develop a plan for making the given decision (or class of decisions) that
adequately addresses all the cardinal decision issues, and then budget
resources to ensure that coverage.

This principle should be familiar to anyone who allocates
resources. The core idea here is the same that managers use for
dealing with the expenses of any project. The project is broken
down into its essential elements and a budget is built to cover
the costs of all those elements. In this case, the plan covers how
a decision will be made, and the elements are the resolutions of
the cardinal decision issues.

Principle 4: Minimization
Seek the lowest costs for adequate decision issue coverage.

Again, this is a version of a principle any good manager observes with other kinds of investment. In the case of decisions, remember to factor in both material and emotional costs. There are myriad ways of minimizing decision costs; imagination is the main constraint. One common and effective tactic is to shift decision modes, for example, by making loan decisions via rules (perhaps executed by computer) rather than from scratch for every application that comes along. Or consider the shift from individual to collective modes. Studies have suggested that because of responsibility diffusion and (even false) impressions of security in numbers, assigning decisions to groups rather than individuals can greatly reduce the distress associated with many business decisions. Consider, for instance, the difference between being the sole person who decides who is fired in a painful downsizing and being part of a committee charged with the same responsibility.

Or consider the agency mode. It is obvious that every manager must delegate some decisions to subordinates simply to avoid being overwhelmed. Less obvious is an important "delegation cost principle": *Every decision should be pushed to the lowest capable ranks.* So, for example, it would be an unconscionable waste of resources to have a plant manager make a decision that could be made competently by a clerk. Yet violations of this principle are all too common, as in the case of Jim Forest at Superior Processing, described at the start of this chapter.

Once it is somehow settled who (or what) will make a particular decision and resources are set aside for the mission, the process of reaching that decision can begin in earnest. Typically, the first order of business is determining which prospective actions the deciders will actually consider and which will never occur to them. That is the province of the options issue, the subject of the next chapter.

CHAPTER SUMMARY

Companies have at their disposal numerous means for deciding. The mode issue deals with one class of means, those summarized in the mode tree. At every branch of the tree, the choice of modes can be either more or less appropriate for producing an effective decision. The investment issue deals with a second class of means: resources, both material and emotional. Too heavy an investment means that a decision is, by definition, deficient in terms of the process costs criterion. Too little investment creates problems for one or more of the other cardinal decision issues.

The wisdom with which companies use the decision means they possess can have marked impact on the quality of company decisions and, hence, company fortunes. Tables 4.2 and 4.3 summarize some of the principles and techniques you can use to improve how deciders in your company address the mode issue and the investment issue in making particular decisions.

Questions for Consideration

1. What is the most vivid instance you can recall, from firsthand experience, when a company was hurt by its bungling of the mode issue? How would you account for what the company did? Suppose you were in a position in the company similar to the position you hold now. What is the single thing you could do that would have the best chance of preventing similar incidents in the future? Now answer the same questions as they apply to the investment issue.

2. A prominent consultant was once asked: "How much should a company spend making an important business decision?" His response: "I always recommend the '10 Percent Rule.' So, if the decision is about an expenditure of $100,000, then the company should spend roughly $10,000 making the decision. If the expenditure would be $10,000, then making the decision should cost $1,000. And so on." What do you see as the strengths and weaknesses of the 10 Percent Rule?

Table 4.2. **Managing the Mode Issue**

Key Mode Issue Challenges	Specific Recommendations
Choice Point 1: Authority	
▪ One decider or more?	▪ Compare collectivity gains to losses.
▪ Which individuals?	▪ Select per decision track record.
▪ Which group leader and members?	▪ Select leader per decision group management skills; select members per cardinal issue coverage requirements.
Choice Point 2: Work Assignment	
▪ Authorized decider's proficiency adequate?	▪ Promote accurate self-assessment, anticipating overconfidence.
▪ Who (or what) is most proficient?	▪ Keep abreast of available alternatives; request peer manager scrutiny.
Choice Point 3: Work Details	
Primary modes	
▪ Analytic?	▪ Recommend as last resort, given costs; guide per methods for addressing cardinal issues.
▪ Rule-based?	▪ Promote per lower costs, better consistency; anticipate and manage resistance, inflexibility.
▪ Automatic?	▪ Anticipate and prevent development of dysfunctional automaticity; retrain using techniques that interrupt automaticity.
Secondary modes	
▪ Modeling?	▪ Verify model comparability.
▪ Agency, consultation?	▪ Select agents and consultants per track records; compensate per decision process investment principles; search for and correct incentive misalignments.

Table 4.3. **Managing the Investment Issue**

Key Investment Issue Challenges	Specific Recommendations
Resource Classes: ▪ What kinds of resources matter?	▪ Recognize and anticipate costs of material *and* emotional resources.
Investment Principles: ▪ How to prevent excessive costs and inadequate support?	▪ Observe principles of limits, reducible decision risk, decision planning and budgeting, minimization.

Prospecting for Solutions

The Options Issue

Consider three business tales, all based on actual incidents.

Sagging Sales:

Sales at Good as Gold, a midsize specialty retailer, had been sagging for quite a while. Speaking of the sales directors in her area, regional sales manager Leslie Shore mused: "Every time we talk about coming up with new promotions, these guys always come back with the same old stuff. They say, 'I just know this'll work, Leslie. It's worked for me like a charm for years.' Then we give it a shot, and nothing happens. This won't do!"

Settling:

The Fellows Group, a real estate management company, needed to replace its departing chief operating officer, Teresa

□

Hines. Hiring a replacement proved to be a real challenge, mainly because, it seemed, few attractive candidates wanted to move to the city where Fellows was headquartered. Eventually, Fellows had to settle for Garrett Mims, a candidate nobody on the selection committee felt was truly up to the job. This assessment eventually proved to be painfully correct.

The Rush Job:
TechPrint was a small but growing high-tech printer. One day, out of the blue, Lance Black, TechPrint's president, got a surprising call from Ted Zint, the head of Flawless, a large local advertiser. Zint wanted TechPrint to take on a big rush job for Flawless, but only according to the terms Zint laid out. After examining the terms, Black had his doubts: making the deadline would seriously strain TechPrint's resources, assuming it could make the deadline at all. And it seemed unlikely that TechPrint would make a dime off the deal. But Black and his partners took the job anyway, expecting that it would lead to more and better jobs later. Once the work was under way, Flawless kept changing the specifications. And when the project was finally done—late—Zint was still unhappy, declaring: "Never again!"

The common denominator of these stories is poor resolution of the options issue, Cardinal Decision Issue 4:

What are the different actions we could potentially take to deal with this problem we have?

Clearly, a possible solution to a decision problem cannot be pursued if it is unrecognized as an option. In each story, there was at least one unrecognized alternative that was superior to the course of action actually taken. By definition, then, the decision in question was ineffective, specifically with respect to the rival options criterion. For instance, as I will describe later, Leslie Shore and her sales directors eventually discovered promotion schemes that far outperformed all the ones they had come up with themselves. Their reaction after those discoveries highlights deciders' overriding fear in connection with the options issue: overlooking good alternatives. (*"That's* what we should have done," they say, "but it never occurred to us!") Your challenge as a decision manager is to help the deciders in your company avoid experiencing the same kind of dismay. More positively, you will want to foster the best possible resolution of the options issue. The place to begin is with the criteria you should use in assessing how well a particular approach handles this issue.

■ Appraisal Criteria

Appraising the various approaches deciders take to the options issue is not as simple as it often seems. That is because there are two pertinent criteria, not one, as people typically assume: inclusion and waste.

The Inclusion Criterion

The inclusion criterion speaks directly to the overriding concern that people have about decision options: overlooking good alternatives. For any decision problem, we can speak of the entire collection of alternative actions recognized by the deciders as the "consideration set." An approach to the options issue is effective with respect to the inclusion criterion *if the consideration set contains the ideal alternative, or at least ones close to it.*

By definition, the ideal option is the one that, in terms of aggregated outcomes, is superior to any other option that might exist. The dismay felt by the leaders at the Fellows Group stems from their suspicion that they did badly with respect to the inclusion criterion. ("There *must* be people out there who could do this job better than the ones we've identified.")

The Waste Criterion

The second criterion is one that people often overlook. Suppose that, by some miracle, Fellows had been flooded with hundreds of candidates for the vacant COO position. This would not be an unmixed blessing. Some of the candidates might be up to the job, but the vast majority of them almost surely would not be. Somehow, somebody would have to wade through all the candidates and figure out which ones to discard out of hand, which ones to consider seriously, and then which ones to aggressively pursue. All of this would make the decision process highly expensive in terms of both material and emotional resources (recall the investment issue). The material costs would include the direct and opportunity costs of having people read dossiers and interview candidates (those people's salaries and the revenue they fail to generate while neglecting their normal duties). The emotional costs would include not only the aggravation of having to perform this difficult work but also the friction generated as committee members work through the inevitable disagreements between those who adamantly oppose Candidate X and those who swear that Candidate X is the company's savior. Worse, in a sense, all these expenditures are wasted on candidates who never actually join the company.

This last point brings up the waste criterion: an approach to the options issue shines with respect to the waste criterion *if it avoids needlessly consuming resources on finding, creating, or appraising inferior alternatives.*

Imagine that, as a decision manager, you get a group of deciders to resolve the options issue perfectly with respect to a major decision. This would mean that they consider only a single alternative—the best. For instance, if you had been managing the Fellows COO search, there would have been only one candidate, one who would have performed the job better than anyone else in the world. Notice that this resolution is perfect with respect to both criteria: it includes the ideal option with absolutely no wasted expenditures on inferior choices. It is, in fact, a perfect decision. Of course, perfection is generally too much to expect. Moreover, typically the inclusion and waste criteria are in opposition: generating more alternatives in an effort to include the ideal one means spending (and thus wasting) more resources creating the pool and evaluating what is in it. So your mission as a decision manager is to strike an effective balance by getting deciders to direct their attention toward options with good potential and to expend minimal resources doing so.

■ Common Approaches to the Options Issue

One solid strategy starts with what you see the deciders in the company doing naturally as they seek to address the options issue. Then appraise what you see against both the inclusion and waste criteria, since there is little assurance that the deciders will have done that themselves. After that, using a variety of principles as well as everyone's ingenuity, craft refinements that achieve improvements on each dimension. Or else persuade the deciders to move to altogether different approaches that are clearly superior in those respects. Table 5.1 summarizes some of the most common approaches around, most of which you have probably seen in your own office. The following sections consider them in turn.

Waiting

The waiting approach clearly does well on the waste criterion: doing nothing is cheap. The problem is that this tack often does very badly on inclusion. Hiring provides good examples. The most suitable candidates for high-level positions, such as COO at the Fellows Group, seldom nominate themselves, partly because

Table 5.1. **Common Approaches to the Options Issue**

Approach	Instruction and Example
Waiting	Instruction: "Let's just see what comes along."
	Example: Posting employment ads and simply waiting for applicants
Exhortation	Instruction: "Try harder! Think!"
	Example: Urging sales directors to work harder at creating new promotion schemes
Invitation	Instruction: "If and when a good idea comes to mind, please let us know."
	Example: Factory floor process improvement suggestion programs
Consultation	Instruction: "Let's find somebody who's an expert at this sort of problem."
	Example: Contracting with a consulting firm to recommend sensible merger partners
Emulation	Instruction: "What's worked for similar problems?"
	Example: Using the same Web designer as competitor Consolidated uses
Exhaustive Search or Generation:	Instruction: "Leave no stone unturned! Consider every possibility!"
	Example: Systematically searching directories for every fastener supplier in business
Brainstorming	Instruction: "Let's meet, kick some ideas around, and try to stimulate one another's imagination."
	Example: Having the entire staff meet in groups to craft new uses for the division's leading product
Derivation	Instruction: "Given our aims and how things work, what makes sense for us to do?"
	Example: Designing a wealthy investment client's customized portfolio per the individual's goals and the company's investment model

they are usually content with the high-level positions they already occupy. Thus companies must work hard just to identify such people, usually with the help of headhunters. After the prospects have been discovered, the companies must woo them so they allow themselves to be regarded as candidates. A company like Fellows, with a liability such as an unpopular location, must be prepared to go the extra mile in this courtship.

You will also see the waiting approach in negotiations, where it again fares poorly. TechPrint's Lance Black, for example, responded passively when Flawless's Ted Zint framed his proposal as a take-it-or-leave-it affair, a common tactic used by people who conceive of negotiations as zero-sum games, where one party's gain is the other's loss. Negotiation experts agree that such hard-nosed stances are usually counterproductive for both sides.[1] That was certainly true for Flawless and TechPrint: neither side gained as a result of Zint's hard-line stance and TechPrint's response.

So what is the alternative to playing the waiting game in negotiations? It is more effective to frame a negotiation integratively, as an exercise in collaborative option creation. That is, the goal is to create options that, as much as possible, satisfy the interests of both parties, only some of which, generally, are diametrically opposed. So instead of simply waiting for Ted Zint's proposal and then responding yes or no, Lance Black would have done both sides a favor by insisting on a discussion resulting in an agreement to proceed—or *not* proceed—that better served the interests of both companies.

The possibility of refusing to proceed brings attention to another key options concept in modern negotiation best practices—the BATNA, or Best Alternative To a Negotiated Agreement. Ideally, before even beginning a negotiation, each party should determine its BATNA, the best thing it could do if there were no agreement with the other party. Had Lance Black and his partners followed this principle, they would have thought hard and creatively about what they might do to advance Tech-Print's interests instead of closing a deal with Flawless. Then, if the discussions with Ted Zint could not beat that BATNA, Black should have been instructed to politely walk away.

One obvious benefit of BATNAs is that they reduce the odds of bad agreements. They also reduce negotiators' anxiety, since negotiators know their limits and have fewer worries about how others on their side will feel about what they achieve. Most pertinent here, the search for BATNAs can turn up valuable new options for the company independent of prospective negotiated settlements.

Exhortation

Urging deciders to work harder at coming up with options can undoubtedly lead to more alternatives. In effect, exhortations are incentives: "Work harder!" translates to "If you work harder, that will make me happy, and I will in turn do good things for you, which will make *you* happy." And countless studies (as well as common sense) say that incentives work. But things can get sticky depending on what deciders believe they are being rewarded for doing—via exhortations or any other means, including pay. Such beliefs can easily surprise managers. ("But *that's* not what I meant!" is a not uncommon cry of anguish after a failed incentive program.) Generally, people take the easiest way out in order to earn a promised incentive. Often this means just doing more of what they have already been doing. At Good as Gold, for example, Leslie Shore's sales directors seem to have responded to her urging by simply recycling their old promotion ideas, only faster. If Shore wanted *different* ideas, she would have done better to promise incentives for *new* ideas. ("Give us something way out there, something nobody's ever done before!") But even that better-targeted incentive would have had minimal effect if her sales directors had no idea *how* to come up with such ideas. The moral is that incentives can be useful, but other approaches are needed to increase not only the size of an option pool but the chance that it will include good alternatives.

Invitation

A broad, standing invitation for recommendations, as in a company suggestion program, is a fine way to exploit the collective coverage idea discussed in Chapter Four. The chances of generating a much wider range of options by including many people in the effort are even greater, however, if the people who work intimately with the problems in question take the invitation seriously.

This last consideration brings up a major hazard of suggestion programs. If your company installs a suggestion program, you might well be flooded with ideas, but only a few of them are likely to be worthwhile. So someone will have to keep telling people, in effect, "Your idea has no merit." How would *you* feel hearing that all the time? You might be inclined to suspect, "This whole thing is a sick joke. The bosses just pick the ideas of their favorites." Or, more charitably, you might say, "The chances of my ideas being implemented are so low that it's not worth my while bothering to submit them." If enough people feel this way, the suggestion program will die a quiet death.

You have three main ways to enhance the value of suggestion programs as tools for generating worthwhile options:

- Create a system for appraising ideas that employees will see as fair and objective, accompanied by routines that say, "Sorry, not this time" in graceful, sensitive ways.
- Reward recommendations in proportion to their ultimately demonstrable value to the company.
- Include compensation in your reward system for thoughtful suggestions, even if they are never enacted.

Consultation

One advantage of the consultation mode of decision making discussed in Chapter Four is that consultants are a source of recommended alternatives, that is, potentially useful options. (Here, I include under "consultants" not only professional consultants but anyone whose opinion is sought for a particular decision problem.) For this reason, consultation can be an exceptionally good way of meeting both the inclusion and waste criteria. After all, a decision problem that is new to one person might be old hat for a well-chosen consultant, who can quickly zero in on a small set of promising alternatives. At Good as Gold, for example, Leslie Shore ultimately hired a consultant, Geoff Lang, who was able to recommend several promotion schemes that he knew had worked well in other companies. These schemes eventually proved their mettle at Good as Gold, too.

Clearly, the key is choosing good consultants. The principles for picking consultants discussed in Chapter Four apply here. In particular, these are the two most critical guidelines:

- Refuse to select a consultant until you have track records to inform that selection; recognize that every consultant will make a persuasive presentation.
- Search for and compare several potential consultants; they are hard to appraise in isolation, since they all seem good.

When deciders do use a consultant to help with the options issue, it is wise to insist that the consultant provide several options for the decision problem, not just one—something consultants often try to do. A consultant who gives you only one option is actually an agent; that is, you have effectively turned the decision problem over to the consultant to solve entirely, something your company should never do casually.

Emulation

Emulation simply means imitating a practice that has worked well in similar situations. In most companies, for example, customer complaints are rarely completely novel. It would be both haphazard and wasteful for a clerk to start from scratch in figuring out how to deal with every complaint as it occurs. It is more sensible to consider the options that have worked before in similar cases. This kind of emulation is a variant of rule-based decision making, and it is precisely what some companies wisely have clerks do. An example is an upscale food market that provides specific options for clerks to consider when customers complain about a lack of freshness (such as "Let me help you get your money back," and never, "Really? Show me"). Modeling, as when your company offers the same employee benefit package options it learns are customary in your industry, represents another variety of emulation.

When feasible, emulation excels in terms of both the inclusion and waste criteria: it gives you attractive options for little expense. The main drawbacks are the ones discussed in Chapter Four with respect to the rule-based and modeling modes of decision making generally. For instance, some situations truly *are* novel, and applying an inappropriate rule can be disastrous.

Exhaustive Search or Generation

Search refers to situations in which the alternatives already exist someplace, for instance, potential employees and store locations. *Generation* applies to circumstances where options must be created, as in product development or strategy. Managers are so fearful of missing good options that it is routine to hear them say, "We've got to consider every alternative, folks!" The result is exhaustive search or generation efforts, ones intended to identify virtually every option—or at least huge numbers of them.

The strong suit of exhaustive search and generation efforts is inclusion: the vast option pool that is assembled has a very good chance of capturing workable alternatives. The Achilles heel of the approach is waste. Conducting exhaustive search and generation exercises is enormously expensive. And appraising the results in search of the proverbial needle in the haystack is even more costly. A company can easily become swamped.

When deciders in your company insist on exhaustive methods—as they sometimes undoubtedly will—you can improve the process by calling attention to the waste issue and suggesting specific ways to manage the costs. For example, you can argue for the wisdom of *limited exhaustiveness* (an oxymoron, I know). What this means is simply doing an exhaustive search within a thoughtfully circumscribed range. No one at the Fellows Group, for instance, would think to waste time searching the ranks of General Mills plant workers for promising COO candidates. Yet we do often cast our nets much more indiscriminately than makes sense in terms of the waste criterion. Before conducting an exhaustive search, therefore, the deciders should do rigorous research on the probable locations of good options. The search can then be designed to exhaust those high-probability sites.

Another way to manage costs is to exploit contemporary technology. At the search stage, for instance, Web search engines can uncover multitudes of options for many decision problems. In a similar vein, be on the lookout for devices such as *shop bots,* automated routines that constantly scan the Web for products that meet a buyer's specifications and can even be instructed to make purchases when they identify qualifying items.

Some companies are exploiting technology to help at the appraisal stage as well. A good (if controversial) example is software that reads résumés and screens out job applicants whose résumés omit essential qualifications.[2]

Brainstorming

Brainstorming is a firmly ingrained part of business culture. When virtually any puzzle arises in a company, you can practically count on hearing somebody propose: "Why don't we brainstorm this for a while?" In practice, what people typically mean by brainstorming is the rather loose technique sketched in Table 5.1. But as originally conceived by Alexander Osborn in the 1950s (and as studied in research), brainstorming entails four specific instructions:

- Effort: "Create lots of ideas."
- No inhibitions: "Include wild ideas. Don't hold back."
- No criticism: "Don't criticize other folks' ideas."
- Piggybacking: "Try to build on others' suggestions."

The "effort" instruction is simply the exhortation idea discussed before. The injunctions against inhibitions and criticism are based on the assumption that many of our best ideas never see the light of day because we are too aggressive in our self-censorship or because we fear looking stupid to others. The piggybacking instruction is motivated by an intuition about synergy, that other people's ideas plant seeds in our own minds that then grow into significantly better ideas in their own right.

These expectations are all plausible. Yet hard supporting evidence is scant, and as a decision manager you should consider refinements or alternatives to conventional brainstorming that appear to achieve the intended aims more effectively. "Electronic brainstorming" (EBS), for example, is conducted on networked personal computers, typically in the same room.[3] Instead of voicing their ideas in an open discussion, participants keyboard them anonymously into the network, where they appear to all the other participants. Studies have shown that inhibition arising from the fear of looking dumb is significantly weaker in EBS than

in face-to-face brainstorming. Another reason EBS is so productive is that it does a better job of capturing ideas before they are
forgotten. You can surely recall having a terrific idea pop into
your head while someone else was speaking, only to have it disappear by the time you got the floor. Since participants in EBS
can enter their ideas into the network simultaneously, there is
no need to wait for turns.

Although the brainstorming synergy idea feels right, it
might well be an illusion. In fact, studies have suggested that
when we are listening to others' ideas, for a while, at least, it is
especially difficult for us to formulate ideas that are significant
departures from the ones we are hearing. This is possibly one of
the reasons that conventional brainstorming has consistently
been found less productive than the "nominal group technique"
(NGT). In this method, participants are asked to generate ideas
working in isolation. As an illustration, Leslie Shore might ask
each of her sales directors to compile their own lists of new promotion ideas alone, perhaps not even knowing that the others
were asked to do the same thing. Another likely reason that
NGT is more productive than conventional brainstorming is that
participants do not have to share floor time and so have more
time to actively add to the pool of ideas (a time-on-task advantage enjoyed by EBS as well).

One last consideration: Studies have demonstrated that
people tend to be more creative when they are in positive, even
silly, moods.[4] (But it's important to note that such moods are no
help with more analytic tasks, such as appraising options, the
aim of cardinal decision issues discussed later.) So, regardless of
the specific techniques you use when trying to come up with alternatives, it is good to lighten the atmosphere first. (Tell a few
jokes, if you are good at that sort of thing.) On the mood dimension, face-to-face brainstorming has an inherent advantage.
As you have probably noticed in your own experiences, brainstorming sessions are often enjoyable, not unlike parties. This is

undoubtedly one reason you normally have little trouble getting people to participate.

Derivation

Deciders sometimes feel that it is reasonable to seek to create only a single option—the best—and they then try to do just that. They believe that they can derive that best solution to their decision problem from their understanding of how things work in the situation at hand. ("If we know enough to figure out precisely what the right answer is, why should we waste our time considering anything else?") They see the situation as analogous to what a calculus student does when solving a function maximization problem.

For some closely circumscribed decision problems, the derivation approach does indeed make sense. Examples include operations management problems that are accurately represented as linear programs that lend themselves to common optimization algorithms. But the derivation approach is suspect in many of the contexts where you will see it being attempted. Consider, for instance, a unit that has been given the go-ahead to build a new facility, but must now decide on its specifications (a construction decision problem, in the language introduced in Chapter Two). Routinely in such situations, the deciders devise a single set of specifications based on considerations such as what unit members think they need in order to do their work. Or take the case of Company A trying to decide on the bid it will offer to acquire Company B (an evaluation decision). Typically, such a bid is based largely if not solely on a financial theory–driven asset valuation model applied to the particulars of Company B. Yet another example would be the development of a plan for launching a new product or service.

Most business decision situations are too complicated and messy to warrant great faith in deciders' ability to flawlessly figure out in their heads the single best solution to a decision problem. As an analogy, suppose you want to build an addition to your house. You relish the chance to plan "exactly what pleases *me.*" Yet I can virtually guarantee that, after conversing with you for a while, a skilled architect could sketch a plan that leaves you admitting, "This is better than anything I could have ever even *imagined.*" This "Designer Effect" highlights our limited ability to create the best option even when it seems we know everything that matters.

The bottom line is that you should seek to persuade deciders in your company to resist the urge to derive the single best solution. Despite the impression that doing so would be pointless, they would do well to apply the "3+ Rule" discussed in Chapter Four: acquire at least three distinct, independently developed alternatives. As the work of Kathleen Eisenhardt has suggested, the resulting decision process may well be faster, not slower.[5] Part of the reason seems to be that it is difficult for deciders to sign off with confidence on just a single option, since that option is hard to appraise in isolation. ("How do we know that that's good enough?") When there are several alternatives, the deciders can at least say that the selected option is better than the others. Moreover, in the event that the favorite option fails to pan out, the deciders know they have backups they have already thought through.

Going Beyond

When deciders handle the options issue especially well, the results go beyond alternatives that are merely adequate. We see surprising actions that compel us to say, "Wow, that was inspired!" The previously discussed refinements to common options issue approaches will improve the odds of this happening. But several complementary tactics add to those odds significantly: using several of the common approaches in the same decision episode; assuring that even brainstorming groups include individuals with expert knowledge of the area; actively soliciting people whose perspectives deviate from the company paradigm; and sharply segregating option generation from option appraisal, since the two activities demand distinct, even incompatible, capacities and dispositions. But once the options are on the table, the decision gears should indeed shift to appraisal, starting with the anticipation of option consequences, the focus of the next chapter.

CHAPTER SUMMARY

Managing the options issue well amounts to assuring that two things happen: the pool of recognized options includes the ideal option, or ones close to it; and the process of assembling and sifting through that pool wastes minimal resources. These criteria provide a way for decision managers to assess and refine the various approaches deciders take to the options issue. Table 5.2 summarizes the main recommendations covered in this chapter.

Table 5.2. Managing the Options Issue

Key Options Issue Hazards and Challenges	Specific Recommendations
Neglect of what matters	Direct attention to inclusion *and* waste criteria
Shortcomings of firmly ingrained, customary approaches	Appraise common approaches as they naturally arise (waiting, exhortation, invitation, consultation, emulation, exhaustive search or generation, brainstorming, derivation) for inclusion and waste; refine; replace as warranted
Contentedness with barely acceptable options	Complement common approaches with multiple techniques, substantive expertise, contrary perspectives, appraisal segregation

Questions for Consideration

1. Recall a significant case in your business experience when deciders chose some particular alternative and shortly thereafter discovered that a superior option had been available all along but was overlooked. How would you account for that breakdown in the deciders' handling of the options issue? In a position like yours, what is the leading thing a manager could do to change the company's decision practices to reduce the odds of similar future errors?

2. Your boss gives you the following mission: "We've been using brainstorming a long time now. I need you to evaluate what we've been doing." How do you go about your task? In particular, what measures of adequacy do you plan to assess and then report to your boss, and why?

6

Anticipating Outcomes

The Possibilities
and Judgment Issues

Secure Savings Bank got into the ATM card business late.
To buy time for working out the bugs in its operations, every
card was given a 12-31-1999 expiration date. Later, there
was concern that this might run afoul of Year 2000 computer
glitches. So during 1999, the company decided to extend all
expiration dates to 12-31-2000. All cardholders received
letters asking them to replace their cards at their leisure
sometime during the year 2000. New Year's Day, 1-1-2001,
was a Sunday, and thus Monday was a legal holiday in the
United States also. When scads of cash-hungry customers
tried to use their ATM cards on New Year's Day (and the
next day too), they discovered that their now-expired cards
were worthless. On Tuesday, January 3, bank personnel were
stunned and overwhelmed by irate customers.

O nce deciders settle on a potential solution to a decision problem, all kinds of things might happen as a consequence. Some of those outcomes serve the interests of the beneficiaries of the decision well, but others, as in the Secure Savings ATM case, do not. Clearly, anticipating all the significant outcomes of a particular course of action would allow deciders to decide more wisely—among other things, avoiding the kind of debacle that occurred at Secure Savings.

Anticipation of outcomes has two aspects, which are reflected in the possibilities and judgment issues. This chapter considers what you can do as a decision manager to increase the odds that deciders will successfully resolve these issues in the course of making important decisions.

■ The Possibilities Issue

The first aspect of anticipation is the possibilities issue, Cardinal Decision Issue 5:

> What are the various things that could potentially happen
> if we took that action—things they care about?

The "they" in this question refers to the beneficiaries and stakeholders for the decision. The core concern is that the beneficiaries will be blindsided by adverse outcomes the deciders never considered in their reflections about the potential consequences of a decision. It is not that the deciders thought about those outcomes and dismissed them as unlikely; the possibility of those outcomes never even crossed their minds. As in the ATM incident at Secure Savings, this complete lapse makes things even worse than otherwise because the affected parties have had no opportunity to prepare for a nasty experience or even to brace themselves for the impact.

Often, simply bringing to mind a potential occurrence would be sufficient to get deciders to choose a different course of action. That is why, after the fact, deciders who have done badly by the possibilities issue often confess that they feel stupid. ("We would *never* have made that decision if we'd even *considered* that possibility. How could we have overlooked it?") At Secure Savings, for example, if it had occurred to someone that New Year's Day fell on a Sunday, and that lots of customers would not have replaced their ATM cards as requested beforehand, the bank could easily have decided to change the expiration date to 1-3-2001. But such oversights sometimes trip up every decider, and so it cannot be a matter of incorrigible stupidity. To help assure that your company is not blindsided by adverse decision consequences, you need to recognize how and why oversights occur, and what you can to do to prevent them. This starts with realizing that these oversights come in two varieties, momentary and fundamental.

Momentary Oversights

In a case of momentary oversight, the deciders overlook a possibility that probably *would* have dawned on them eventually, given enough time. At Secure Savings, for example, someone might well have noticed the New Year's Day problem before it was too late. It is just that, after the decision to change the expiration date to 12-31-2000 was made, no one gave the matter any further thought.

Momentary oversights crop up for several main reasons: aim contentment, physical prominence, immediacy, capacity limits, associations, and stress. Each of these oversight contributors has recognizable features and established countermeasures.

Aim Contentment
Recall that every decision episode begins with an aim, the specific goal the deciders seek to achieve. Unfortunately, all too often, once the deciders discover an option that would indeed

achieve their aim, they pursue it—end of story. The problem is that company actions typically lead to many other consequences beyond achieving or failing to achieve the deciders' aim. Sometimes those side effects can be so bad that, in the aggregate, they make the selected alternative worse than other available options.

Such premature aim contentment appears to have been the main culprit in the Secure Savings case. Changing card expiration dates to 12-31-2000 neatly achieved the bank managers' intention of buying time for working out ATM operation bugs. Having chosen an option that met the need they recognized, the managers then failed to further scrutinize the possible effects of pursuing that option.

One effective tool for reducing the odds of premature aim contentment is the application of O-P-O (Option-Possibilities-Option) cycles. They work like this: The deciders first come up with an option (O) that appears to achieve their aim. Instead of stopping there, they then perform exercises designed to identify other beneficiary- and stakeholder-significant potential outcomes, that is, possibilities (P). Such exercises could include simple adaptations of the option generation tools discussed in Chapter Five, such as brainstorming. The deciders use the results of these exercises to broaden their decision aims, for example, to include avoiding the problematic possibilities they have identified. Then they look for additional options (O) that meet these broader aims, again perhaps with the help of the option-generating approaches sketched in Chapter Five. The deciders repeat O-P-O cycles until no new worrisome possibilities emerge. At that point, they have an option that not only meets their original aim but avoids all the untoward possibilities they have been able to envision.

The O-P-O cycle approach almost certainly would have prevented the grief experienced at Secure Savings. Probably in the first cycle, someone would have said something like, "You know, we can't count on all our customers renewing their ATM cards by a certain date just because we send them a letter. We'd better make sure the change goes into effect on a day when the bank will be open."

Physical Prominence
Think back to the job interviews you had at your company before you were offered your current position. If your experience was like most people's, the interviews were a lot like everyday, casual conversations. ("So, how was your flight?" "What interests you about our company?" "You do rock climbing, *too?*" "What do you like about managing people?" "What would you like to be doing five years from now?" "How 'bout them Red Sox?") Your employer got lucky with you, of course, but generally, such "conversational interviews" are shockingly inaccurate job performance predictors.[1] It is easy to understand why in terms of the possibilities issue.

New employees will eventually do an enormous range of things on the job that affect the company's interests, for better and worse. Managers know in advance what many of these significant actions are, yet at interview time they fail to ask questions that would be informative about what the interviewee would actually do in the pertinent circumstances. That is because the flow of ordinary conversations is haphazard, flitting from one interesting topic to the next. The interviewers are thus led to neglect key, knowable facts about job candidates that can easily lead to blindsiding. ("We had no *clue* that he'd behave like *that!*") This is an instance of the misdirection of attention by physically prominent stimuli, such as the fascinating but irrelevant tangents that occur in casual conversation. Like neon lights, these tangents serve as cues saying, "Look here!"

Checklists are an excellent way to combat this source of momentary oversights. This is the basic idea behind "structured interviews," in which a script guides the interviewers through a list of carefully prepared questions designed to uncover information that will help them gauge how a candidate is likely to act in situations that matter to the company. ("Would you please describe for me an instance in which you . . . ?") Research has shown that structured interviews are far more valid than traditional conversational interviews.[2]

Some physically prominent cues, unlike conversational tangents, are not coincidental; they reflect strategic intent. For example, any proposal your company receives from a vendor will purposely highlight the vendor's strengths. If the document mentions the vendor's weaknesses at all, they will be given short shrift. There is therefore a good chance that the managers in your company will never even think about the possible problems those weaknesses might create for your company if the proposal were accepted. The 3+ Rule discussed earlier requires that a manager who receives a proposal should solicit at least two other proposals, too, before making a decision. The competing vendors will generally have different strengths. Their proposals will direct attention to different considerations that might matter to the company, thereby counteracting momentary oversights due to physical prominence.

Immediacy

Deciders sometimes overlook significant potential outcomes because those outcomes will surface, if at all, only in the long term. In the personal arena, imagine a young manager who gets a new job and hurriedly buys a house that is quite sufficient for his current needs. But three years later, he discovers that the house is too small for the family that he and his new wife are starting, and its design does not permit an addition. Moreover, he learns that home values in the neighborhood historically appreciate very little. So if he moves his family, he will suffer a big financial hit. The potential for all these things could have been foreseen. But, out of sight in the distant future, they were also out of mind when the young manager bought the house.

The most promising preventatives for such immediacy-based momentary oversights are two types of decision customs. First are look-ahead customs. For example, it is good for every company to establish a tradition that, before any major, nonroutine decision is finalized, someone says: "Before we sign off, let's ask ourselves: 'What would doing this mean for us a year from now, five years from now . . . ?'" Then there are "What then?" customs, which speak to chains of cause and effect that play themselves out over time. So, for instance, you would work to institutionalize a practice whereby, before significant, out-of-the-ordinary decisions, somebody always says, "Before we close on this decision, let's ask, 'What then?' If these possibilities occur, *then* what could happen that we'd care about, one way or the other? . . . And if *those* things happen, what happens after *that?*"

Capacity Limits

Try to do the following arithmetic problem without the aid of paper and pencil:

$$352.17 \times 731.5 + 823.7 - 15.6/4.2 = \underline{\hspace{2cm}}$$

Unless you are a mathematical savant, you cannot solve this problem in your head, even though you know perfectly well how to execute every one of the required operations. Why? As you perform each operation, you attempt to store the results in memory and then move on to the next operation. But by the time you do that, you have forgotten the previous results. You have run up against the capacity limit on what psychologists call "working memory."

Since we are all familiar with this effect, ordinarily we would not even try to solve complicated math problems in our heads. Yet we often think nothing of solving serious, complicated company decision problems (such as establishing new substance abuse policies) that way. The results are momentary oversights. At the point where we say, "OK, that's what we're going to do," that action can easily fail to reflect key factors that have simply slipped from consciousness.

Effective approaches to the capacity limit problem tend to sound overly simplistic. Yet they work, and you should work hard to keep the deciders in your company from dismissing them as frivolous. One approach is collaborative deliberation. Especially if a decision problem is unfamiliar, it is highly risky to have the decision made by one person, no matter how confident the individual is about thinking of everything. After all, the very nature of an oversight encourages overconfidence, since there is no apparent reason for doubt. As the decision manager on the scene, you can insist that two or more people discuss the problem. As with the collective coverage idea discussed earlier, the collective capacity of the group will be considerable even though the capacity of each individual decider is small.

A second approach to the capacity problem is the same as the one we all use when doing arithmetic: physical displays and records, which can be as simple as paper and pencil. As illustrated in Chapter Seven, decision matrices are an especially useful physical display for decision problems. Decision matrices are simply tables or charts that display an array of considerations across various options, as in the product comparison charts you see in publications such as *Consumer Reports.* So, for example, a table might assign one alternative to each column and one factor or consideration to each row. Thus suppose that the choice of a chief operating officer has boiled down to four candidates. Then the hiring committee would list each candidate's name at the head of a column and assign each relevant consideration, such as the ability to lead effective teams, to one of the rows. As the committee reviews the entire matrix, it is hard for any member to forget what any particular candidate is like on any given dimension.

Associations

Suppose that, in her COO interview, candidate Stephanie Garr is so stunning in the image of technical competence she projects that everyone says, "Wow!" Then, for a good while, it will be hard for you, as a member of the selection committee, to think about anything other than technical competence. If you were to make your decision right then, that single consideration would probably dominate your thinking about all the candidates, to the point that other important considerations might not even come to mind.

There are two related reasons for this type of momentary oversight. The first concerns mental associations: we are especially sensitive to things that are associated with whatever is already in mind (technically, in working memory). Hence, candidates who are discussed immediately after the Garr interview have an inordinately good chance of being scrutinized with respect to their technical competence. The other reason for neglect concerns capacity limits. When one class of considerations (such as ones associated with technical competence) have captured our attention, they effectively crowd out other, unrelated considerations (such as social skills), which we then overlook.

One simple way to help deciders protect themselves from association-based momentary oversights is to promote another decision custom: waiting. Although deciders will often be tempted to make a decision immediately after gathering all the information they feel they need, it is safer, as a rule, to resist that temptation. Instead, the deciders should hold off on finalizing their decision, in the meantime doing lots of other tasks. This will allow their mental apparatus to clear, which increases the chances that they will give all the relevant considerations their due when they return to the question. (This is the psychological wisdom behind the idea of "sleeping on the problem.")

Stress

Many circumstances tend to induce stress in deciders: time pressure, high stakes, interpersonal conflict, fatigue, and so on. The most firmly established effect of stress on mental functioning is that it restricts the scope of attention.[3] This is known to reduce the creativity essential for discovering good options. Whether and how this also prevents the decider from recognizing important possibilities depends on several things.

Figure 6.1 illustrates the "habit model of stress constriction." It shows the effects of different stress levels on the factors that a decider takes into account when deciding. The center of the concentric circles, the point denoted "H" in both panels of the figure, represents the class of facts to which the decider habitually, under relaxed conditions, is most likely to pay attention. As stress increases, attention narrows toward these habitually favored considerations. This effect occurs for every decider, expert or otherwise.

Now, one thing that it means to be an expert is that one tends to pay close attention to the truly important things and ignore everything else. Thus, as represented in Panel A of Figure 6.1, the most habitually attended facts for an expert are also the ones that are most critical (C) for deciding well (hence, H = C). Therefore, initially, at least, the expert's decision effectiveness actually improves with increased stress because the decider is even less likely than usual to be distracted by irrelevant information. Effectiveness reaches a peak when the scope of attention matches the range marked "Essential," which encompasses all the considerations that are required for the ideal decision. Further stress beyond that point, though, cuts into the bone, causing even experts to overlook things they need to consider in order to decide well.

Panel B depicts the corresponding situation for non-expert deciders. The key difference, as denoted by the distant location

A. Expert Decider

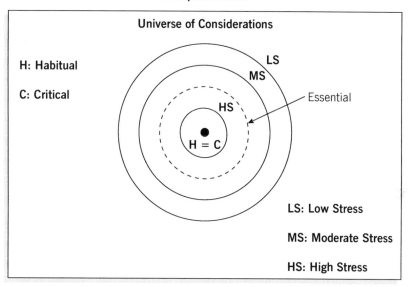

B. Non-Expert Decider

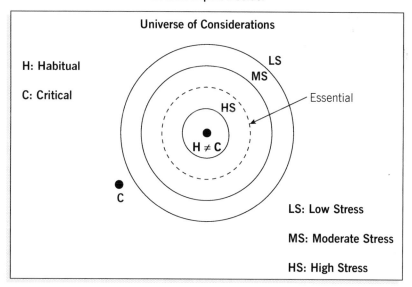

Figure 6.1. Stress Effects on Attention to Decision-Relevant Considerations

of the C in this panel, is that the habitually attended considerations are far from the truly critical ones (H ≠ C). Indeed, the focal considerations are likely to include ones that are useless if not harmful for good decision making. As stress increases and the decider's attention narrows, the odds that the decider will take critical factors into account grow even worse. That is, the quality of the non-expert's decisions steadily deteriorates under increasingly stressful conditions.

A second moderator of how stress affects attention is personal significance, or value. According to the "personal significance model of stress constriction," the higher the stress, the more attention goes to factors that have special significance to the decider. The word *personal* underlines the fact that these factors not only vary from one individual to the next but may or may not be particularly important to the company. Nevertheless, research has documented one across-the-board implication of the personal significance effect: most deciders will become increasingly risk averse as stress increases. This follows from the fact that stress highlights potential losses as well as the general psychological principle that the average person is hypersensitive to losses, as compared with gains.

Three key approaches will help you deal with the effects of stress on deciders' neglect of important considerations: collaboration, reliance on experts, and reliance on stress-resistant individuals. In a crisis-like situation (for instance, a bitter, raucous negotiation session), all of your company's deciders are likely to have severely constrained scopes of attention. Maintain a sacred rule in such situations that no one, not even the most expert decider, makes a big decision alone. Instead, several people *must* decide collaboratively. Also in crisis situations such as worksite accidents, since your non-expert deciders (for example, newly promoted managers) are especially likely to have their attention restricted to the wrong things, it is prudent to send them to the sidelines and allow them to observe the experts at work. Finally, it is useful to exploit the fact that, although some people's constitutions cause them to fall apart under stress, others are largely stress resistant. Indeed, some such people, called *hardy*, even consider situations that most of us regard as stressful to be pleasant challenges.[4] If certain units in your company (say, your customer complaint office) chronically demand decisions under stress, it would be wise to investigate known means of identifying and recruiting such people for service in those units.

Fundamental Oversights

When oversights are momentary, deciders are inclined to say of an overlooked consideration, "It just slipped my mind." But in cases of fundamental oversights, they say things like, "I wouldn't have thought of that in a million years." More generally, *fundamental oversight* means that the chances of a particular consideration coming to mind are nil no matter how long the deciders are allowed to ruminate. Two major contributors to fundamental oversights with respect to possible outcomes are common—personal inexperience and sheer novelty.

Personal Inexperience

Sometimes deciders fail to think about certain potential decision outcomes because they have never experienced anything resembling them, even though countless other people have done so. Health care provides excellent examples. Consider a patient who has developed breast cancer and faces the decision of how to have her illness treated. Although millions of women, unfortunately, have been in that situation, for that patient, the situation is virtually unique; she faces possible outcomes of different treatments unlike anything she has ever encountered. Or take the case of mergers. As common as mergers are, the chances are good that the executives and managers of any given company have personally been involved in only a couple of them, if that.

The obvious antidote to personal inexperience as a cause of fundamental oversights is to call upon the experiences of others. This can mean casting a wide net, because a very serious possible outcome might also happen to be rare. Thus a cancer patient relies on her physician's knowledge of the outcomes of thousands of cases, as represented in studies in the medical literature—and at that, she would be wise to get a second and even a third opinion. A vice president of a major manufacturer told me that, relying on the same idea, before his company agreed to merge with another firm, it commissioned a study of the three hundred largest mergers in history. The aim was to discover what bizarre, unpleasant, and off-the-wall things *could* happen so that the deal could be structured to avoid them.

Sheer Novelty
Some decision situations are new to everybody, as in the case of emerging technologies like genetic engineering or radical business environments such as deregulated energy markets. And some situations that superficially appear routine, are, upon closer inspection, quite special. For instance, recent research has established a number of principles that come into play in all negotiations. Yet most negotiators also concede that every negotiation entails unique circumstances (such as the personalities and their histories) that make it hard to predict all the possible outcomes. The sheer novelty of such situations virtually assures that deciders, left to their own devices, will overlook significant possible occurrences.

Companies have two avenues for reducing the odds of fundamental oversights in novel situations:

- *Theory consultants:* Unlike consultants who are valuable because of their experiences in similar situations, theory consultants do not rely on having seen or even heard of specific solutions to your company's decision problems. Instead, their value lies in understanding the theory of how things work in the given arena. So, for example, if your company were contemplating entering a new kind of deregulated market, you would do well to hire as a consultant an economist who is an expert on deregulated markets generally.

- *Simulations:* Existing theory often has severe limits. That is why some companies wisely complement theory consultation with simulations in their efforts to anticipate the kinds of things that could happen if they were to pursue completely novel solutions to the decision problems they face. Simulations of deregulated energy markets in university experimental economics laboratories are a good illustration. They can vividly demonstrate the bizarre, including exploitative, things that are *likely* to occur in real life regardless of what theory says *should* occur. My personal simulation favorites, though, are the role-plays of labor negotiations reported by Scott Armstrong at the Wharton School. Armstrong's studies have shown that such simulations are far more accurate in forecasting negotiation outcomes than even recognized experts are likely to be.[5]

■ The Judgment Issue

A proposed information technology reorganization at Vanguard Manufacturing called for making system development a central headquarters function but attaching systems analysts to local installations, close to line operations. At one point, IT consultant Jack Shields gave the management board an estimate that the reorganization would deliver technology solutions in half the time they took previously and at half the cost. The board approved the reorganization. Two years later, it was apparent that technology solutions would not be achieved faster and that costs would be even higher than before.

Central to the Vanguard Manufacturing IT case was the judgment issue, Cardinal Decision Issue 6:

> Which of the things that they care about
> actually would happen if we took that action?

Whereas the possibilities issue involves identifying the potential decision outcomes that could occur, the judgment issue deals with the next step—drawing conclusions about whether particular potential outcomes will in fact occur. Thus, Jack Shields's predictions that solution times and costs would be halved by the IT reorganization were judgments. More formally, in this context a *judgment* is an opinion as to what was, is, or will be the actual state of some decision-relevant aspect of the world. Most decisions rest at least partly on judgments in this sense. At Vanguard, for example, the anticipated reductions probably made the proposed reorganization irresistible. But there is another inescapable fact of decision life, too: the accuracy of judgments imposes a ceiling on decision effectiveness. That is, decisions can be no better than the judgments driving those decisions allow them to be. At Vanguard, the effectiveness ceiling was low indeed.

Perspective on Judgment and Decision Management

Your goal as a decision manager is to help make sure that the judgments that guide your company's decisions are as accurate as possible. You can have a positive impact on deciders' judgment accuracy through every one of the four types of activities in the decision management portfolio: influencing specific decisions, supervising decision routines, shaping decision practices, and providing decision resources. But the most critical activity is the first—affecting specific key decisions. Besides being important in its own right, what you do in facilitating these decisions indirectly affects what you can achieve in the other arenas, too. The sound judgment practices that you get people to employ when making critical decisions can serve as models for practices throughout the company. And the decisions themselves might well be ones that guide widely used decision routines (for instance, rules for selecting company investments).

So the discussion here focuses on judgments in situations where the company faces a decision problem of some consequence. Picture yourself, for example, as a member of the management board at Vanguard Manufacturing, pondering the IT reorganization proposal. In the language of the mode tree introduced in Chapter Four, your board starts at Choice Point 2: Work Assignment. The board could make the decision relying solely on its own judgments. Alternatively, it could take a hybrid approach. That is, although the board anticipates making the ultimate decision itself, it might consult others for judgments that would inform that decision. There are, therefore, three problems to pursue: whether to consult others; if so, how to use consultants effectively; and how the deciders can enhance the accuracy of their own judgments.

Whether and Whom to Consult

The decision about whether to consult others is a make-or-buy decision: "Should we ourselves make the judgments we need for this decision, or should we buy them?" Just as for any other make-or-buy decision, the key considerations are comparative quality and price. On the Vanguard management board, you and your colleagues would (or should) reason something like this:

> To make a sound decision, we need good judgments about how this IT reorganization would affect our solution times and costs. Are there people (or devices) out there who could give us judgments with accuracy that's so much better than our own that it would more than offset what we'd have to pay for them?

If the answer to this question is yes, then consultation is the way to go; otherwise, it is not. The logic here is fine. The problem is that companies seldom try to apply it and, perhaps partly because of that, they seldom have the required facts. Hence your role.

Overconfidence

Research has consistently shown that, under certain conditions, deciders are overconfident in their judgment skills. So there is a good chance that your management board at Vanguard would be overly confident in its own ability to accurately predict how much the reorganized IT structure would reduce solution times and costs. This would, of course, discourage the very idea of consultation from coming to mind. And even if that avenue does come up, it is easily dismissed: "Nah, we don't really need to do that."

As was true of the overconfidence problem discussed in an earlier chapter, the issue here is not inflated egos, in the sense of people thinking that they are smarter than they really are. Studies have shown that, instead, it is a matter of people's failing to see reasons to doubt their competence. Few of us entertain illusions that we could fix our color TV sets if they broke down; one peek into the cabinet makes our ignorance patently obvious. Things are different when deciders ponder the deceptively difficult yet seemingly nontechnical judgment problems entailed in most business decisions, including Vanguard's IT reorganization.

The most sensible thing to do is err on the humble side: simply assume that the deciders in your group—including you—are more confident in their judgment abilities than is truly warranted. Concretely, this means working to establish a norm that, when facing a new, unfamiliar decision problem, deciders in your company routinely plan to enlist the judgment services of others unless there is a very good reason not to do so.

Potential Consultants

Finding and picking consultants is merely another decision problem. Thus all the ideas discussed earlier apply, including the options approaches reviewed in Chapter Five. Naturally, the deciders in your company would want to seek consultants who have reputations in the pertinent area, for instance, in information technology for your IT reorganization problem. Invariably, deciders start with personal connections ("I know a guy . . . "). This is fine as far as it goes, but it is often suicidal to stop there. The 3+ Rule applies with a vengeance in selecting consultants. Insist on screening at least three potential consultants, each recommended by independent sources, people who themselves tend to think differently. As with options more generally, this will prevent the deciders in your company from asking plaintively: "How can we tell if she's good enough? Compared to what?"

Accuracy Verification

How, exactly, should deciders pick among their judgment consultant candidates? Research suggests that deciders are likely to base their selections on criteria that can be problematic.[6] Undoubtedly, reputation will be a key consideration. But what impresses others and therefore dictates people's reputations? Major determinants of such impressions include the appearance of confidence and precision (for example, saying, "Our model predicts a savings of 52.8 percent" rather than, "Oh, we'd guesstimate savings of about half"). They also include the consultant's ability to offer convincing explanations. ("She makes so much sense!") The drawback of impression drivers like these is that they are easy to fake, and consultants have powerful incentives to do just that.

You will never convince the deciders in your company to ignore these considerations; do not even bother trying. But you should insist that they also apply another fundamental principle, the Behavior Prediction Law:

The best predictor of future behavior is past behavior.

In the present context, this rule says that deciders need to examine records of the candidates' judgments and how well they matched actual occurrences. Thus, before basing a major decision on Jack Shields's forecasts of 50 percent reductions in IT solution times and costs, your Vanguard management board would have a specialist statistically evaluate the correspondence between Shields's past forecasts and the truth. That evaluation would then be compared to similar evaluations of the judgments of other potential consultants (and ideally evaluations of the deciders' own judgments).

Be warned, though, that gaining access to these records will be difficult. Most consultants will be taken aback that you would even ask. (How often have you known of financial analysts who volunteer records that would allow you to appraise the accuracy of their earnings or price forecasts?) Be gracious in your requests, but persist nevertheless.

Using Consultants

Suppose that the authorized deciders have elected to solicit consultant judgments. There are better and worse ways of drawing on what the consultants have to offer. It is useful to consider them in the context of several key questions that arise.

How Many Consultants?

Typically, companies hire a single consultant for any given decision problem. Part of the motivation, of course, is cost. Another is that deciders see no point in having more than one consultant. They reason: "We've picked one of the best if not *the* best there is. So if we hired another consultant, we'd be wasting our money since that second consultant would be either inferior or redundant to the first." One problem with this argument is that the accuracy of the judgments rendered by even the most expert consultant is far from perfect. Another, related problem is that even the most expert of experts disagree with one another surprisingly often. (Companies are generally unaware of this because they seldom bother to solicit judgments from more than one consultant.)

You would be wise to encourage the deciders in your own company to break from tradition and, whenever feasible, hire at least two independent judgment consultants for a major decision problem. "Independent" means not only that they come from different firms but also that they tend to think differently and work separately in arriving at their judgments for the problem at hand. Thus, besides Jack Shields, your Vanguard management board would solicit IT solution time and cost estimates from at least one other expert who arrives at those assessments by different means and without consulting Shields in the process. Depending on several factors, including how you synthesize what you get from your various consultants, the increase in accuracy can be substantial, more than enough to offset the increased expense. Why? One major reason—which your deciders will easily appreciate intuitively—goes back to the notion of collective coverage. That is, the different consultants derive their judgments on the basis of considerations that only partly overlap with one another. When combined, those judgments do a better job of taking into account everything that matters. So, while Jack Shields might emphasize user responsiveness in his IT solution time estimates, independent consultant Susan Shaw might zero in on headquarters-field communications.

How to Resolve Disagreements?
You will often see discrepancies between the judgments your deciders get from different consultants. What then? You have two options, mechanical and deliberative.

In the *mechanical* approach, the deciders derive a composite judgment using a formula, typically an average of some kind. Suppose that, while Jack Shields's estimate for the reduction in IT solution time is 50 percent, Susan Shaw's is only 20 percent. Then a composite forecast that is a simple average would be (50 percent + 20 percent)/2 = 35 percent. As simple-minded as averaging might seem, research has shown that it often does an excellent job of improving accuracy.

In the *deliberative* approach, there is some form of review and perhaps even a discussion of judgment inconsistencies. The idea is to understand why the disagreements exist and thereby get closer to the truth on the basis of logic. One version of this approach is a variant of the "Delphi method." Applied to the Vanguard IT problem, Jack Shields and Susan Shaw would submit their forecasts along with their rationales. Each would examine and deliberate the other's work and then be given the opportunity to revise his or her own in light of that review. This process continues until it is obvious that no further revisions are likely. If the consultants do not arrive at a common judgment, an average might be computed. In the traditional Delphi method, the consultants would never interact face-to-face and might not even know one another's identities. But, properly managed, there can be advantages to actual discussions.

How to Ask?

Recall that this is how Jack Shields articulated his forecasts regarding the proposed Vanguard IT reorganization: "Solution times and costs would be cut in half." Suppose that, although a reduction by half was indeed his best single estimate, in his heart of hearts, Shields also felt that there was a 15 percent chance that solution times would actually *increase*. Would the deciders on your management board want to know that? Of course. The reality of judgment is that it is rare for consultants (or anyone else) to be (justifiably) absolutely sure about what is going to happen. Yet, almost without exception, companies ask their consultants to give them flat-out, unqualified assertions: "So, what will sales be?" "Will they finish by June or won't they?" "Would she succeed in this job?" And, of course, the consultants comply. After all, expressing doubt makes them look less competent to their clients, and they know that.

You would therefore do your company a favor if you helped establish a custom whereby consultants are routinely asked to express their judgments in terms of likelihood. Probability formats are best, although words such as "good chance" or "unlikely" are better than nothing. For instance, your management board would do something like present Jack Shields with ranges of post-reorganization IT solution times like these: increased by more than 50 percent, increased up to 50 percent, decreased up to 50 percent, decreased by more than 50 percent. Shields would then report his probability judgments that the actual average solution time would be in each of those intervals, say, 10 percent, 15 percent, 50 percent, 25 percent, respectively. One good thing about judgments expressed in probability judgment format is that there are good, well-developed ways of keeping track of and analyzing consultants' accuracy.[7]

How to Pay Consultants?

As a rule, when companies engage consultants for their judgments, compensation is not tied to the accuracy of those judgments. To motivate properly directed diligence, it should be. Suppose that Susan Shaw is contracted for her opinions about the proposed Vanguard IT reorganization. If at all possible, part of her pay should be in the form of a bonus that is eventually awarded—or not—according to the correspondence between her forecasts and what eventually occurs. There are good, defensible ways of doing this.[8]

What About Devices?

Increasingly, companies have at their disposal various devices—typically computer programs—that can provide them with judgments the same way that people do. In our terms, these devices are potential consultants, too. Illustrative programs actually in use include ones that make sales forecasts, predict loan defaults, and provide medical diagnoses. As much as possible, your company should appraise and use devices the same way it appraises and uses human consultants, with an emphasis on their accuracy and their costs. Over and over, studies have demonstrated the superior accuracy of various devices. For instance, one report indicated that whereas physicians' accuracy at predicting cancer recurrence was no more than 50 percent, the corresponding rate for a certain computer program was 90 percent.[9] Neither patients nor health system administrators would sniff at such a difference. Nor would they ignore the fact that using such programs is generally cheaper than relying on doctors.

When effective devices are available, why should your company not simply use them to replace human consultants? For several reasons, including the acceptability issue (Chapter Eight): depending solely on machines just makes some people uncomfortable. Another, perhaps more defensible, reason rests on the same principles that argue for using more than one human consultant. Human and machine consultants have different and complementary strengths and weaknesses. The strong suit as well as the Achilles heel of human consultants is their vision. A computer program necessarily renders its judgments solely on the basis of the specific facts that someone enters into the program—no more, no less. In contrast, a human consultant can look at the given situation, notice all sorts of things (say, a patient's apparent will to live), and then integrate those facts into a judgment. If those facts are systematically related to the truth (for instance, whether patients will survive certain treatments), in principle this is a decided advantage over a rigid computer program. But if those facts are independent of the truth, then taking them into account can damage accuracy severely. The strong suit of computer programs is their reliability or consistency. Studies have repeatedly shown that a prime reason that humans lose in judgment contests with machines is that the humans are inconsistent. As one famous researcher put it, "People have their days," whereas machines do not.

The wisest course is to use devices as consultants in tandem with human consultants, pursuing the tack described before for using multiple human consultants. Thus, one thing that the deciders in your company can do is acquire judgments from both your devices and your human consultants and then combine them mechanically, for example, in an average. As an instance of the deliberative approach, when there is a large discrepancy between the devices and humans, this could be taken as a signal for an investigation pursuing questions such as, "Why did this happen? What did the machine see that we didn't, or vice versa?" Part of your responsibility as a decision manager is to ensure that your company's deciders understand their devices sufficiently well to discover the answers to such questions. All too often, companies simply buy devices and have minimal comprehension of how they work.

Enhancing Deciders' Own Accuracy

Even when your company's deciders consult others for judgments relevant to their decisions, they naturally cannot resist using their own judgment as well. Thus every member of your management board at Vanguard Manufacturing has a personal opinion about what solution times and costs would probably be under the proposed IT reorganization, and Jack Shields's estimates will not completely override that opinion. You therefore have the challenge of taking measures to make sure that the deciders' own judgments are more accurate than they would be normally. A functional approach to this task is addressing factors that suppress accuracy. Researchers have learned a lot about such suppressors. The following sections discuss several that figure especially prominently in common business decision situations and that you can attack with great effect.

Suppressor 1: The People Involved
The accuracy of the judgments that drive the decisions ultimately reached by company deciders can be suppressed by

who those deciders happen to be. The problem has three key aspects:

- *Numbers:* There may be too few people involved in the judgment process. No one is surprised that accuracy potential generally increases with the number of people participating. But it often does surprise us to learn how large the effects usually are.

- *Redundancy:* There may be too little intellectual diversity among the participants in the judgment process. The increase in accuracy afforded by involving more people in the judgment process is achievable only to the extent that participants' opinions are not redundant. If Chris and Lee always agree in their opinions, then combining their judgments cannot possibly allow us to predict anything more accurately than using just Chris's judgments. Incidentally, another hazard of redundancy is that it lulls deciders into overconfidence. After all, if everybody agrees on something, then it must be right, right? Wrong.

- *Skills:* Another prerequisite for accuracy seems to go without saying: The people making the judgments must themselves be skilled judges, in the same way that worthwhile consultants must have demonstrable accuracy. Ordinarily, deciders have little idea how good their own accuracy is, let alone that of their fellow deciders. (By the way, research has shown that knowledge about the subject matter in an area, for instance, information technology, though necessary, is far from sufficient for making accurate *judgments* in the area.)

The prescription for these problems goes back to the mode issue (Chapter Four): You should work toward an ideal whereby, when decision groups are being assembled in your company, those groups have decent numbers of intellectually diverse people whose judgment accuracy for the problem at hand has been documented.

Suppressor 2: Social Dynamics

When a decision-making group at your company is discussing things in an effort to arrive at judgments to inform the final decision, the dynamics of that discussion can inhibit accuracy. One obvious hazard is ridicule and fear of ridicule. As noted in Chapter Five, admonitions against criticism in brainstorming groups and the anonymity of electronic brainstorming are intended to cope with this problem. You can adapt these approaches in judgment discussions, too. Another hazard mentioned earlier was the "shared information effect": instead of talking about things they are uniquely equipped to contribute to the discussion, group members instead talk about things known by everybody in the group. To recap, an effective way for you to deal with this problem is to force people to talk about judgment problems beyond the point where they *think* they have reached informed consensus.

Suppressor 3: False Indicators

Like everyone else, deciders sometimes hold false beliefs about what is or is not indicative of the truth in some situation. For example, they might believe that having certain kinds of experiences is predictive of how well people perform as service managers because that seems logical to them. Yet an examination of the objective data might uncover no connection at all. Not surprisingly, such false beliefs wreak havoc with judgment accuracy. One technique for reducing the odds of reliance on false beliefs is called "devil's advocacy." Whenever a group member makes an assertion about the predictive utility of some fact, have another member of the group vigorously play the role of an antagonist who challenges that claim.

Accurately anticipating the effects of decision alternatives on various external occurrences, such as task completion times and costs, is clearly essential for effective decision making. But that is seldom enough. Among the remaining tasks are ones that focus on what makes decision making most special—value, including the fact that one beneficiary might easily despise outcomes another beneficiary loves. I turn to considerations like these in the next chapter.

CHAPTER SUMMARY

Any option that a company's deciders might choose to pursue will result in a host of outcomes that affect the company's interests. Thus effective decision making depends on how well the deciders can foresee those occurrences. The possibilities issue concerns anticipating what company-significant outcomes could conceivably happen, while the judgment issue is about predicting whether those potential occurrences will in fact happen. Tables 6.1 and 6.2 summarize the steps you can take as a decision manager to improve how deciders in your company resolve these issues.

Table 6.1. Managing the Possibilities Issue

Key Possibilities Hazards and Challenges	Specific Recommendations
Momentary Oversights	
▪ Aim contentment	▪ O-P-O cycles
▪ Physical prominence	▪ Checklists; 3+ Rule
▪ Immediacy	▪ Look-ahead customs; "what then?" customs
▪ Capacity limits	▪ Collaborative deliberation; physical displays and records (including decision matrices)
▪ Associations	▪ Repeated, spaced deliberations
▪ Stress	▪ Collaborative, distributed deliberation; expert deciders; stress-resistant deciders
Fundamental Oversights	
▪ Personal inexperience	▪ Others' collected experiences
▪ Sheer novelty	▪ Theory consultants; simulations

Table 6.2. **Managing the Judgment Issue**

Judgment Issue Approaches: Key Hazards and Challenges	Specific Recommendations
Seeking Consultants	
■ Overconfidence in own judgment	■ Assume overconfidence and compensate
■ Appointing inaccurate consultants	■ Follow reputations; compare three or more candidates; verify accuracy per track records
Using Consultants (Including Devices)	
■ How many consultants?	■ Employ two or more independent consultants
■ How to resolve disagreements?	■ Synthesize judgments mechanically, with formulas, or resolve disagreements by discussion of substance
■ How to ask for judgments?	■ Request likelihood opinions
■ How to pay consultants?	■ Make compensation at least partly contingent on accuracy
■ How to best use devices?	■ Use devices in tandem with people, taking the best of both
Enhancing Deciders' Own Accuracy	
■ Accuracy suppression by the choice of participants	■ Rely on several people, not one; intellectually diverse people; people with documented good accuracy
■ Accuracy suppression by poor social dynamics	■ Guard against ridicule; act against the shared information effect
■ Accuracy suppression by dependence on false indicators	■ Verify predictive utility of facts, including via devil's advocacy

Questions for Consideration

1. Review in your mind cases where you have seen companies confront highly consequential instances of the possibilities and judgment issues and fail. Take one example of each variety. In your estimation, what elements of the companies' approaches played the most significant roles in those failures? What changes in company practices would greatly reduce the chances of similar failures in the future? What actions could a person in your position take to move the company measurably toward those changes?

2. Devil's advocacy is an effective and even popular technique in the United States. But because it emphasizes open conflict—even if only simulated conflict—it is less popular in Japan, where such disagreement offends cultural norms for harmony. Devise a technique that plausibly would achieve benefits similar to those of devil's advocacy but would be more acceptable in Japanese culture.

Accounting for Taste

The Value and Tradeoffs Issues

Eighteen-hour days were routine for ViewTech's founders,
Lane Woods and Mia McCoy. They sought the same dedica-
tion in everybody they brought on board. ("Every one of us
is excited about creating something new here, right?") Even
the most junior service employees were expected to be in the
building from 8 A.M. to 6 P.M., and they got no extra pay if a
task required work beyond even those long hours. Several
months later, ViewTech's clerical workers rebelled. They
complained to the state labor department, charging that the
demand for uncompensated overtime was illegal. The state
agreed, applied costly sanctions, and promised to keep an
eye on ViewTech.

The ViewTech case highlights the one thing that, you will recall, distinguishes decision making most sharply from more general problem solving: the personal significance that people attach to decision outcomes—their tastes. The cardinal decision issues discussed in this chapter involve the two distinct, though related, aspects of personal significance that matter most in decision making.

■ The Value Issue

The first critical element of personal significance is the focus of the value issue, Cardinal Decision Issue 7:

> How much would they *really* care—
> positively or negatively—if that in fact happened?

That is, part of effective decision making entails accurately anticipating how particular parties to a decision will feel about the potential outcomes of various decision options. At ViewTech, for example, an important part of Lane Woods and Mia McCoy's thinking was an expectation about how their employees would feel about putting in extra hours for no extra pay, that is, how they would value the experience. Clearly, they misjudged those feelings, and the resulting decision did significant damage to the company.

A Judgment Perspective

As the last observation suggests, the value issue is actually a special case of the judgment issue discussed in Chapter Six. What is special is the focus: deciders are making "valuation judgments"—judgments about people's likes and dislikes. As with judgments generally and so aptly illustrated by the ViewTech incident, valuation judgment accuracy imposes a ceiling on decision effectiveness. In your decision manager role, you can adapt many of the ideas discussed in connection with the more general judgment issue to valuation judgment tasks (for instance, using multiple consultants). However, valuation judgments also involve special challenges that set them apart.

Whose Values?

The first complication you face concerns who the people are whose values your company's deciders need to judge. It is easy to simply overlook some of those people, a problem that arises again in Chapter Eight in connection with the acceptability issue. So one way to contribute significantly to more effective resolution of the value issue is to give deciders a simple means for checking whether they have neglected people whose values warrant attention.

Recall from Chapter Two that most decisions involve numerous parties. The parties whose values need assessment are the beneficiaries and stakeholders. The beneficiaries matter because it is their interests and desires the deciders are trying to serve. For the ViewTech overtime decision, the beneficiaries included the owners and, in the view of Woods and McCoy, the affected employees themselves—included in "Every one of us. . . ." The stakeholders matter because if they are displeased, they are likely to take actions that harm the beneficiaries. At ViewTech, the employees assumed the role of stakeholders, too, as did the state labor department.

There are two simple elements to the prescription for making sure the values of beneficiaries and stakeholders are accurately assessed in any high-stakes decision situation:

- *Inventories:* The deciders should exhaustively bring to mind and then explicitly list all the significant beneficiaries and stakeholders for the decision.

- *Checklists:* The deciders should use the completed inventory as a checklist for ensuring that they make defensible assessments of how every party on that list would value potential outcomes.

Deciders are often unpleasantly surprised by the number of different beneficiaries and stakeholders whose values they must assess. "Do we *really* need to do all this work?" they will complain. Let them be the judges. But remind them of the risks of oversight.

False Consensus

As Chapter Six demonstrates, it is useful to frame judgment problems as make-or-buy propositions: deciders can either make needed judgments themselves or they can get them from other people. In the case of valuation judgments, a widespread psychological phenomenon likely to tip the balance too far in the make direction is "false consensus," the belief that other people hold views more like our own than they really do.[1] False consensus almost certainly played a significant and costly role in the ViewTech case. The founders' words—*"Every one of us is excited about creating something new here, right?"*—betrayed their erroneous assumption that everybody in the company shared their personal values.

False consensus hits valuation judgments with a double whammy. First, false consensus can discourage deciders from seeking others' input, that is, pursuing the buy option. ("Everyone will pretty much feel the way I do, so what's the point?") Second, deciders' specific valuation judgments will be biased toward their own personal tastes. ("Who could *possibly* dislike this?")

As a decision manager, simply assume that false consensus will color all decision deliberations. Then promote conventions that counteract its effects. The norm should be that, especially for major decisions, the bias is toward the buy option. Before finalizing any action, deciders would be expected to question their assumptions about what beneficiaries and stakeholders like and dislike and to seek corroboration from others. At ViewTech, before settling on a company-wide salary pay scheme, Lane Woods and Mia McCoy could, for example, float the idea past people they know at other companies, or perhaps call on a consultant knowledgeable about attitudes at numerous companies.

A big reason that people differ in what they value is that their situations lead them to have different personal needs. Victor needs and hence likes minivans because he has three kids; Tyler does not because he is childless. False consensus can easily survive because we do not readily appreciate others' circumstances and therefore how their needs and tastes differ from our own. That is why role-play exercises in which deciders, in effect, try to live others' lives—for instance, experience potential customers' workdays—can also improve valuation judgments.[2]

Candor and Self-Insight

It only makes sense, it seems, that the people to consult about valuation judgments should include the beneficiaries and stakeholders themselves. After all, who would know better than they what their own likes and dislikes are? By this logic, Lane Woods and Mia McCoy would have asked all prospective or current ViewTech employees how they felt about a company-wide salary (versus hourly) pay scheme. What could possibly go wrong? Two things: a lack of candor and a lack of self-insight.

The main reason beneficiaries and stakeholders are sometimes reticent about their own values is that they believe candor hurts them. Picture Bob Fisk being interviewed by Mia McCoy for a position at ViewTech. Fisk knows perfectly well that he would loathe having to work overtime for no extra pay, but he is desperate for a job. So when Mia asks, "How would you feel about that, Bob?" he does not respond: "Well, frankly, Ms. McCoy, I'd just *hate* it." People also camouflage their feelings because they hope to avoid being rude or creating a scene. It would certainly be uncomfortable for Bob Fisk to say, "Ms. McCoy, I think that asking people to put in extra hours without pay really stinks." So he holds his tongue. And if he gets the job offer but has other options, he politely declines, offering excuses other than his disdain for the pay scheme. Either way, Mia McCoy is never the wiser.

Now imagine Mitzi Shavers, another job candidate at ViewTech. In her interview, Shavers says that she "wouldn't mind" uncompensated overtime, and she genuinely means what she says. Yet three months after taking the job, she is so unhappy about its long unpaid hours that she is actively seeking employment elsewhere. Shavers has experienced a self-insight failure, a discrepancy between how she *thinks* she values something and how she really does.

Self-insight failures happen for a number of reasons. When a person has never encountered some particular outcome, *entailment errors* are a common contributor: the outcome in question entails experiences that the person simply failed to recognize while making a valuation judgment. At the moment when Mitzi Shavers said that she would not mind working long hours without extra pay, she was not envisioning what eventually happened to her: tedium, fatigue, resentment, and complaints from her family.

When self-insight failures occur for things that are not new to us, it sometimes reflects the fact that our brains, broadly speaking, have two parts that communicate with each other only imperfectly.[3] The *affective* part deals with our feelings, including our likes and dislikes. The *cognitive* part is concerned with thinking functions like memory and deduction. To illustrate, suppose that we experience deep satisfaction with some event, such as a terrific meal. Because the cognitive part of the brain has only imperfect, indirect access to the affective part of the brain where the satisfaction actually occurred, it can only infer what was *probably* responsible for that satisfaction. And that inference can be mistaken. Thus, we might conclude that it was the food itself that accounted for our sense of pleasure at dinner, whereas the true explanation was some combination of the food, atmosphere, and company. So when we order the same dish on another occasion, in a different atmosphere and with different companions, we are disappointed. Similarly, although Mitzi Shavers might have been fully content in an earlier job that involved unpaid extra hours, that contentment probably derived from factors other than the time at work and lack of pay.

Yet another big reason for self-insight errors is that people's values often change over time. In fact, values frequently are highly volatile. One explanation concerns people's reference points. How we feel about things depends heavily on our standards of comparison, and those standards change easily, with surprising results. If, for example, Mitzi Shavers thinks that uncompensated overtime is the norm in ViewTech's industry and area, then not being paid extra may be OK with her. But the instant she learns that ViewTech is the only company of its kind in the region using an all-salary pay scheme, the burden immediately feels painful.

One kind of reference change that has special significance is the *endowment effect:* when we are given something that is even mildly appealing, our liking for it skyrockets immediately. This is plausibly a major reason that once people acquire some privilege such as a bonus payment, it can quickly become regarded as a right and, thus, impossible to withhold without a fight. And it is important to remember that people do not expect that they personally are subject to the endowment effect even though they are.[4]

Difficulties with candor and self-insight do not mean that deciders should conclude that asking people how they feel is pointless. There are, instead, two fruitful approaches you can promote:

- *Complementary sources:* Deciders should avoid relying *solely* on what beneficiaries and stakeholders can tell them; they should instead actively seek additional indicators of what people's actual values might be.
- *Compensatory tactics:* Deciders can take specific measures to reduce the effects of candor and self-insight limitations. The single best way to encourage candor is to have questioning done by transparently neutral parties.

At ViewTech, Lane Woods and Mia McCoy would not personally ask employees how they feel about their own proposal. Instead, a contract consultant selected partly by workers themselves might ask the questions. Simulations, such as trial periods and role-plays, are especially good for helping people get beyond their self-insight limitations. Simulations often make people vividly aware of what outcomes entail, and people literally feel the emotions engendered by what is entailed.

Unpredictability

The expression "There's no accounting for taste!" conveys the popular belief that understanding and accurately predicting people's likes and dislikes is really hard. This belief is justified. As suggested earlier, our feelings about things are subject to a vast array of forces, such as changing reference points, changing needs, satiation, opinions of friends, media messages, and even simply growing older. It only makes sense, then, that no single fact we can learn (for instance, a person's age, gender, or profession) can possibly be sufficiently strongly related to that person's values to permit more than a modicum of accuracy in valuation judgments. Yet two fundamental ideas can help deciders cope with this frustrating unpredictability, the regressiveness and cumulative validity principles.

The Regressiveness Principle

Suppose someone says "We asked, and they say they'd just *love* it!" to describe the way parties to a decision would feel about something, for instance, employees' sentiments about a new work schedule. The deciders should not then decide as if those people really *would* love working on the new schedule. Instead, the deciders should presume that employees' true feelings would be more neutral, close to the average. (The same would apply if the feelings in question were on the negative side.) This prescription derives from the *regressiveness principle.*

Here is how it works: Suppose we know absolutely nothing to distinguish the current case from any other. For example, imagine that we have no details about the proposed work schedule, nor have we asked a single person for an opinion on it. Then by default we would have to predict that employees' feelings about the new schedule would match their feelings about the typical work schedule. The only way we can ever justify a prediction that deviates far from the average is on the basis of solid, highly valid evidence. But when we are trying to anticipate people's values, *no* single piece of evidence is highly valid, including people's own expectations that they will love something. Thus, we should regress our valuation judgments toward the average because of the weak validity of the available information.

The Cumulative Validity Principle

You have never seen an employment test consisting of only two questions, and you never will. Instead, such tests often have fifty items or more. Why? Test designers are exploiting the *cumulative validity principle,* which says that the combined validity of a collection of indicators generally increases with the number of indicators included in that collection. Although any single test question has only a slight correlation with job performance, the validity of the total, fifty-item test score can be substantial indeed.

Nobody is surprised by the basic idea underneath the cumulative validity principle. What does surprise people, though, is how sharply the validity of a collection of weakly valid facts increases as more of them are added to one another. People's values can never be predicted to a high degree of accuracy. Nevertheless, as dictated by the cumulative validity principle, synthesizing several value indicators can yield accuracy respectably beyond the level of chance. Thus, back at ViewTech, Lane Woods and Mia McCoy could have done at least a fair job of predicting employee sentiment about pay practices if they had gathered good amounts of independent evidence.

Intuitive Decision Making

No company committee would sign off on a major decision just because a member says, "I don't know why, but that just *feels* like the right thing to do. So let's just do it, OK?" But many managers will confess to times when they would like to do exactly that: pursue some action on the basis of vague intuitions. Interestingly, research suggests that intuitions can indeed have value as valid early signals. There is growing evidence that, if you have repeated experience making certain decisions, your brain might establish connections that essentially bypass consciousness.[5] Then, when you encounter particular decision situations, your brain in effect rapidly receives subtle signals mediated by the emotions, crudely saying either "Yes, this is a good thing!" or "No, stay away!" Your intuitions, then, may in fact capsulize a great deal of information derived from past experiences, all outside your awareness.

Few managers would openly acknowledge such gut feelings as justification for a decision. But many will be sorely tempted to use intuition as a private rationale and, perhaps, manufacture other, more respectable explanations for public consumption. It is good to promote a different norm on intuitive decision making in the company. Intuition should not be summarily dismissed. Instead, it should be taken as a signal that something may be there. The decider experiencing such an intuition has the obligation to ask *others* to independently seek evidence that corroborates or refutes that intuition. This emulates hard-nosed newspaper editors who demand of their reporters: "Give me two sources."

What About Economic Value?

Invariably in discussions about value, someone says, in effect, "Business is about money—*economic* value. How does that fact of life jibe with all this fluffy talk about 'taste'?"

One answer is simply that *value* has two distinct meanings in business decision making, both of them essential. *Economic value* refers to the objective financial consequences of some business activity, for example, its impact on share prices. Questions about anticipating these consequences are the province of the judgment issue discussed in Chapter Six. The value issue, in contrast, concerns predicting subjective likes and dislikes—a separate but also vital consideration.

A second response to the economic value complaint is more specific. For distant beneficiaries such as shareholders, personal value questions are largely moot; economic value is nearly their sole concern. Things are vastly different for immediate beneficiaries, the people whose actions create economic value, and for stakeholders, whose engagement with the company is often extensive. Money is definitely not the only thing that matters to these parties. As ViewTech's founders discovered, failing to correctly anticipate how a particular decision will engage stakeholders' values can have serious repercussions.

■ The Tradeoffs Issue

Chambers Brothers needed a supplier for a critical component, and Kate Minetti was the manager responsible for leading the effort to select that supplier. Minetti and her team assembled a large pool of potential suppliers and, after initial screening, reduced the pool to four: Zephyr, Darwin, Parallax, and Fenton. They also worked hard to identify the relevant considerations that might distinguish those suppliers. The consideration list was huge, but after careful review, it was reduced to twenty factors, such as engineering capability, location, and on-time record. Then things got complicated. Every supplier was good on some dimensions while not so hot on others. For instance, although Zephyr's engineering was superb, its location was inconvenient. Kate Minetti's frustration was understandable: "Oh, man! What should we do? If we want good engineering, we have to give up location. If we want reliability, we have to give up compatibility. And on and on."

At the heart of Kate Minetti's dilemma was the tradeoffs issue, Cardinal Decision Issue Eight:

All of our prospective actions have both strengths and weaknesses. So how should we make the tradeoffs that are required to settle on the action we will actually pursue?

Virtually every decision episode eventually gets to the point where the deciders must confront critical tradeoffs like those faced by Kate Minetti and her colleagues at Chambers Brothers. And, generally, once those tradeoffs are made, so is the decision. The resolution of the tradeoffs issue is ordinarily the point where the deciders say: "We're done. That's what we're going to do."

In contrast to numerous other cardinal decision issues, the tradeoffs issue rarely escapes deciders' attention. People are usually acutely aware of tradeoffs because they are often emotionally taxing, as when, in her despair, Kate Minetti moaned, "Oh, man!" That is why deciders in every company have at least implicit and sometimes explicit routines for dealing with tradeoffs. And when managers are discussing decisions they consider to be bad ones, they seldom explain those failures in terms amounting to "We got the tradeoffs wrong." This all gives the impression that, as a decision manager, you never need to worry about how your company's deciders cope with tradeoffs; all is well. That impression is false.

The discomfort deciders typically experience when facing difficult tradeoffs suggests that, whatever approaches companies commonly use in tradeoff situations, there simply must be better ways of reducing that distress. And it is unfortunately easy for deciders to assume they have made the right tradeoffs even when they have not, thereby reaching decisions they believe to serve the company's interests when they actually harm them. Thus your challenge is to help provide assurances that the tradeoff customs the company already has in place are up to the task and, if they are not, refine or replace them.

The MAUT Technique

At Chambers Brothers, the Minetti team applied a technique often called "multiattribute utility theory," abbreviated as MAUT and pronounced "mowt." This is convenient because MAUT and similar methods (including the "analytic hierarchy process") are fairly popular tradeoff tools that are worth considering for your own company if they are not used already. They also allow for good illustrations of ways a decision manager can refine current tradeoff practices. The method starts with a decision matrix, a table with options as columns and various nonredundant dimensions or considerations characterizing those options as rows. Figure 7.1 shows a small and simplified excerpt from the humongous decision matrix for the Chambers Brothers supplier

Consideration	Supplier			
	Zephyr	**Darwin**	**Parallax**	**Fenton**
Engineering Capability Rk=1, Rt=30	"Outstanding" 100	"Adequate" 0	"Outstanding" 100	"Good" 50
Location Rk=3, Rt=15	"Poor" 0	"Ideal" 100	"OK" 60	"OK" 60
Compatibility Rk=4, Rt=10	"Seamless" 100	"Ornery" 0	"Decent" 50	"Smooth" 75
On-Time Record Rk=2, Rt=20	"Average" 50	"Excellent" 100	"Good" 75	"So-so" 0
Total Score	5000	3500	5900	3150

Figure 7.1. Decision Matrix and Multiattribute Utility Theory (MAUT) Analysis for the Chambers Brothers Supplier Choice Problem

problem, displaying just four options and four dimensions. (Component price was intentionally excluded since the deciders expected it to be identical for all suppliers.) Abbreviated, the MAUT analysis involved six steps.

Step 1: Status Assessments. The Minetti team first assessed the status of each option (that is, each supplier) with respect to each consideration. For simplicity in communication, the team reduced each assessment to a capsule phrase, such as "Adequate," "Seamless," or "So-so."

Step 2: Status Ratings. The team then attached a 0–100 rating to each assessment. In the particular MAUT scheme employed, a 0 is assigned to the worst level that a particular consideration assumes *in the context of the specific options being compared,* and a 100 is given to the best option in that context. So, for instance, Darwin's 0 on engineering capability does not mean that Darwin has nothing to offer in this area or even that it has the worst engineering capability of all suppliers around. It simply means that Darwin is weakest on this dimension among the four elite suppliers being considered. Similarly, the 100 given to Zephyr means that this firm is tied with Parallax as the best of the four in engineering capability. Intermediate ratings are then assigned to the remaining options according to their apparent distances from the 0 and 100 anchor levels.

Step 3: Importance Rankings. The team next rank-ordered the considerations in importance, from engineering capability as most important (Rank = Rk = 1) down to the interpersonal compatibility of the supplier contact persons and those at Chambers Brothers, ranked last (Rk = 4).

Step 4: Importance Ratings. Next the team rated the relative importance of the considerations. By convention, the least important factor, compatibility, was assigned an importance rating or weight of 10 (Rt = 10). The procedure requires that the remaining factors receive weights proportional to their importance relative to that of the least important factor. So, for instance, engineering capability, with a weight of 30, was considered three times as important as compatibility.

Step 5: Scores. After that, the team calculated a total score for each option. The total score formula in this version of MAUT is:

$$\text{Score} = (\text{Weight}_1 \times \text{Status}_1) + (\text{Weight}_2 \times \text{Status}_2) + \ldots + (\text{Weight}_L \times \text{Status}_L)$$

In this formula, Weight_x represents the importance rating or weight for given factor x, from the first (x = 1) to the last (x = L). Status_x denotes the numerical status rating for the focal option on the corresponding dimension. Thus, the total score for Zephyr was computed like this:

$$Score_{Zephyr} = (30 \times 100) + (15 \times 0) + (10 \times 100) + (20 \times 50) = 5000$$

Step 6: Selection Recommendation. The last step is easy: MAUT prescribes that the decider select the alternative with the highest score. From the Total Score row in Figure 7.1, observe that Parallax was the recommendation in this case.

Outcome × Outcome Tradeoffs: MAUT Reflections

MAUT addresses one of several distinct kinds of tradeoffs common in business decisions: outcome × outcome tradeoffs. In this type of tradeoff, strength with respect to one kind of definite outcome ("We'd get excellent engineering from Zephyr") is cast against (and possibly traded for) strength in another ("With Darwin, we'd get a perfect location"). MAUT provides one particular means for resolving several such tradeoffs, all in one fell swoop. But it is also useful to consider how well MAUT fares as a *good* way of doing this, and how you, as a decision manager, could significantly improve on how the technique is commonly applied.

Anxiety and Disagreement
MAUT can help greatly with two varieties of emotional costs deciders experience: anxiety and disagreement. Anxiety accounts for much of the anguish people associate with tough decisions. ("Is it really *right* for us to be giving up compatibility for location?") MAUT reduces anxiety because it seems to provide a straightforward, easy-to-follow procedure that ends with an unambiguous recommendation: "Do this."

MAUT also helps defuse the interpersonal conflict that often surrounds important decisions. First, the analysis is transparent: starting with the decision matrix, everything is right out front for everybody to scrutinize. Second, all the parties involved can easily see where they disagree, and this can serve to focus reconciliation discussions productively. For example, at Chambers Brothers, a useful exchange might start: "Can you remind me why you think compatibility would be so good at Zephyr?" And, finally, if the parties accept that the MAUT formula is a legitimate means for making tradeoffs, then MAUT can serve as the equivalent of a trusted, neutral arbitrator in a negotiation, where the parties agree in advance: "We'll go by whatever the numbers say."

But although MAUT does indeed reduce anxiety and disagreement, this comfort brings with it a hazard. Often, deciders are *too* comfortable. Their contentment encourages them to be remarkably uncritical about whether the procedure has yielded *proper* tradeoffs, a problem I will return to later in the chapter.

Sacrifice
MAUT cannot directly help at all with a third kind of emotional cost that weighs on deciders faced with tradeoffs, namely, sacrifice. In any outcome × outcome tradeoff situation, by definition, none of the beneficiaries can have their cake and eat it too. For instance, it seems that Chambers Brothers cannot have a supplier with both excellent engineering and an excellent location. MAUT per se takes the options for the decision problem at hand to be givens. Thus, it offers no immediate relief for the person who complains, "I hate giving up *anything*. Do I really *have* to?"

As this complaint suggests, ideally, the best way to deal with tradeoffs is to make them unnecessary. And one way to do that is by finding or creating a "dominating alternative." A dominating alternative is one that is at least as good as every competing option with respect to all the factors that matter, and it is better on at least one of those factors. Seeking such an alternative amounts to reframing a problem with the tradeoffs issue as a problem with the options issue, a problem amenable to the approaches discussed in Chapter Five.

When facing the specter of sacrifice, many deciders feel compelled to redouble their efforts to find a dominating alternative. You will find that MAUT decision matrices often help with this "dominance striving" strategy. First of all, the matrices make sacrifices starkly obvious. Thus, after seeing the Chambers Brothers matrix, Kate Minetti might be so unsettled that she says, "This is awful. Every *one* of these companies has a serious liability. Shouldn't we beat the bushes harder and find somebody who has none of those shortcomings?"

Matrices also make it more apparent exactly what sacrifices each alternative demands and therefore exactly what the deciders need to find in their quest for better alternatives. In fact, in a most common variety of the dominance striving strategy, the deciders seek to transform one of the existing options into a dominating alternative by eliminating its weaknesses as these have been isolated in the MAUT analysis. Taking this tack, Kate Minetti's team might try to work with Zephyr to improve its on-time record and convince it to open a facility closer to Chambers Brothers.

Ignorance
Another valuable service that MAUT provides is making deciders more cognizant of their ignorance. Invariably, when deciders construct a decision matrix, they discover—often to their surprise—that they do not know enough to fill all the cells. Yet this is comforting because the deciders then recognize exactly what they *need* to know. The matrix constitutes a good shopping list of facts they must acquire to inform their decision. It enables deciders to more effectively cope with the possibilities and judg-

ment issues as they arise in the decision at hand. At Chambers Brothers, when the Minetti team began its work, they had no idea how little they knew about the on-time records of the competing suppliers. Finding out took lots of work. In fact, the team required *weeks* to learn everything needed to complete the entire decision matrix, but they considered the investment well spent.

Importance

The total score formula is the mechanism MAUT uses to achieve tradeoffs. And most critical in making the tradeoffs in a specific situation are the importance weights. Consider Panel A in Figure 7.2, which graphically depicts the status ratings for two of the Chambers Brothers supplier options, Zephyr and Parallax. Observe that those alternatives are equivalent (and superb) in engineering capability. But whereas Zephyr is better with respect to compatibility, Parallax is better on location and on-time record. So, if the Minetti team selected Zephyr over Parallax, they would be trading away location and on-time delivery strength in return for compatibility strength. Intuitively, it seems that, if compatibility is sufficiently important, Zephyr's compatibility strength should more than offset its poor location and on-time record, thereby justifying that tradeoff and that choice; otherwise not. MAUT makes this intuition concrete and precise for deciders via importance weights. Recognize, though, that MAUT itself provides no guidance on what the weights (and hence tradeoffs) ought to be. It is inescapably the deciders themselves who must set the weights, for better or worse.

Examine Panel B in Figure 7.2. The white bars show the importance weights originally presented in the Minetti team's decision matrix (in Figure 7.1). Recall that, using those weights, MAUT recommended Parallax over all the other suppliers, including Zephyr. The black bars show the importance weights of manager Andy Mertz, who was not part of the supplier selection team and who told Kate Minetti, "I think the team's weights are

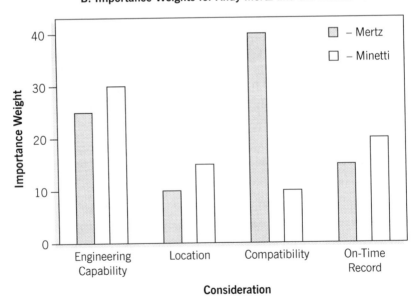

A. Status Ratings for Suppliers Zephyr and Parallax

B. Importance Weights for Andy Mertz and the Minetti Team

Figure 7.2. Status Ratings and Importance Weights for the Chambers Brothers Supplier Choice Problem

all wrong." Observe that, in contrast to the team, Mertz attached very high importance to compatibility, the dimension on which Zephyr outshone Parallax, and little significance to location and on-time record, Zephyr's weaknesses. In fact, the differences are sufficiently great that the Mertz weights lead to a recommendation of Zephyr rather than Parallax; you can easily plug the numbers into the MAUT formula and find that S_{Zephyr} = 7250 and $S_{Parallax}$ = 6225.

The tradeoffs (and, equivalently, the contrasting weights and choices) of the Minetti team and Andy Mertz cannot both be right. Thus, this example highlights three key questions about importance weights in MAUT:

- *Meaning:* What would it mean to say that the deciders got the weights wrong in a particular instance?
- *Explanation:* What explains *why* deciders sometimes arrive at improper weights?
- *Prevention:* How can a decision manager reduce the odds that deciders will assign weights improperly?

The answers depend on whether the concern is with economic importance or personal importance, which I discuss in turn.

Economic importance. In a situation like that facing Kate Minetti's supplier selection team, the focus might well be almost exclusively economic, for instance, on unit production costs. Stretch your imagination and picture four alternative futures at Chambers Brothers, in each of which, respectively, the company has selected a different one of the competing suppliers. The first line in Figure 7.3 depicts the actual unit cost savings resulting from using that supplier. You see, for instance, that in the "Zephyr future," unit costs would be lower by $9, but in the "Darwin future," the reduction would be only $4. The second line reproduces the MAUT scores originally shown in Figure 7.1, based on the Minetti team's importance weights. The third line

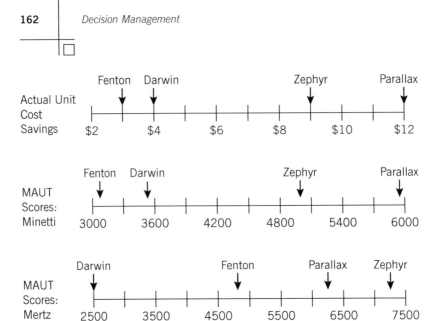

Figure 7.3. Unit Cost Savings and MAUT Scores

shows the corresponding MAUT scores predicated on Andy Mertz's weights. Observe that the Minetti MAUT scores track the order and spacing of the actual cost savings much better than the Mertz scores do.

Implicit in this example is the appropriate meaning of getting importance weights right and wrong in the economic sense. More explicitly and generally:

> Weights are correct to the degree that the resulting MAUT scores are good predictions of what actual economic results turn out to be.

Thus making decisions according to recommendations derived from those scores would lead to better economic returns than otherwise. Clearly, then, the Mertz weights are more wrong than the Minetti weights. Those weights would lead to the selection of Zephyr rather than Parallax, resulting in unit cost savings of $9 rather than $12.

One significant reason that deciders can make mistakes when assigning importance weights is a direct consequence of decision management. In nearly every MAUT application I have seen, the deciders are provided only minimal guidance when given requests like: "Please tell me how many times more important engineering capability is relative to compatibility." To anthropomorphize, when MAUT hears from the Minetti team that engineering capability is three times as important as compatibility, this is how it interprets that report:

> If an improvement in compatibility (for instance, from the worst level to the best) produces an improvement of size X in overall supplier adequacy (for instance, lower costs), then an equivalent improvement in engineering capability would yield an adequacy improvement three times as big, of size 3X.

And MAUT would act accordingly in changing its overall scores. I routinely hear deciders saying things like, "This factor is ten times as important as that one." But when they learn what importance *really* means to MAUT, they recognize that they almost never truly believe that any one consideration is that much more important than any other.

The economic importance of any dimension characterizing decision alternatives has some actual, true value. For instance, at Chambers Brothers, changes in engineering capability would indeed yield improvements that are some particular multiple or fraction of equivalent changes in compatibility. Viewed this way, it becomes clear that assessing economic importance is simply a special case of the judgment issue. So the same ideas discussed in Chapter Six apply here too.

In particular, you can expect deciders to be overconfident in their ability to accurately appraise economic importance. In fact, overconfidence should be severe. Deciders virtually never

get definitive feedback about the validity of their importance assessments. After all, they almost always select only a single alternative and therefore have no real evidence how the rejected
alternatives would have turned out (the "path untaken" problem). Suppose the Minetti team adopted Andy Mertz's importance weights, selected Zephyr, and then experienced cost
savings of $9. Who would know that they would have done sub-
stantially better with Parallax? The team can therefore easily
maintain their belief that the weights they used were just fine.
Moreover, even if they happen to be unhappy with Zephyr, real-
life situations are so complex that it would be easy for them to
misattribute this unhappiness to factors other than poor importance weights. This is why deciders so rarely explain decisions
that turn out poorly in terms of bad tradeoffs.

So when MAUT and similar procedures are used in your
company, as a decision manager you would do well to take three
measures: First, make certain that all the deciders truly understand what they ought to mean by *importance* when they express
importance opinions. Second, when economic value is the concern, frame the task as a judgment problem: the mission is to
make tradeoffs that do the best job of anticipating specified economic returns, such as revenue or cost savings. And finally, exploit all the ideas known to be effective for supporting accurate
judgment generally, for example, using multiple, documented
expert consultants.

Personal importance. For some business problems where
MAUT might be employed, economic concerns are indirect or
distant, if relevant at all; the focus is on personal value. A good
example of such a problem might be deciding which worthy
charities a company will support with its limited resources and
which it will not. Charities differ along many dimensions that
the company's constituencies care about, such as their local
versus national versus international impact, their focus on health

rather than other concerns, and their access to other funds. The basic logic of MAUT remains the same, as does the concept of what *importance* ought to mean. The critical difference concerns the ultimate criterion the decision is intended to optimize. In the case of economic value, the criterion is concrete, something like cost savings. But in the case of personal value, the target is fuzzier, the degree of satisfaction particular people will experience with whatever option is selected. Thus MAUT is, in effect, attempting to make accurate valuation judgments. So, if the overall MAUT score for Charity A is higher than that for Charity B, this is essentially a prediction that supporting Charity A would be more satisfying than supporting Charity B.

Cast this way, it becomes clear that questions of personal importance are actually special cases of the value issue addressed earlier in this chapter. Thus the same approaches discussed there can be applied directly to facilitate better personal importance assessment. The earlier recommendations for managing MAUT applications can be adapted, too. The most useful special recommendation for a decider applying MAUT and similar methods in the personal value arena concerns the people whose values are to be served. Those people need to be explicitly identified. Why? Mainly because, as noted earlier, Person A can easily loathe what Person B cherishes, and hence it is easy for deciders to be wrong when they say things like, "I just know they think that local impact is more important than health impact." The particular beneficiaries ("they") need to be specified, and then their actual values verified.

Noncompensatory Methods for Outcome × Outcome Tradeoff Situations

MAUT is said to be a *compensatory* scheme for synthesizing multiple considerations because strengths and weaknesses with respect to various considerations can compensate for one another.

In Figure 7.1, for example, Parallax achieved the best MAUT score even though it was far from ideal in terms of compatibility. In contrast, noncompensatory methods for synthesizing conflicting considerations do not allow such a thing to occur, because they do not permit the trading of strength on one dimension for strength on another. In effect, they prohibit tradeoffs.

The best-known examples of noncompensatory methods are *conjunctive* schemes, like those common in decision making about loans. Such rules usually take a form like this:

> Make the loan if the applicant has lived
> in the area more than X months, and has collateral
> of at least Y, and . . . ; otherwise, do not make the loan.

By these rules, a loan is ruled out when an applicant falls short on even a single criterion, no matter how fantastic the application might be in other respects.

Are noncompensatory schemes unreasonable? Do they lead to decisions that are more likely to harm beneficiaries' interests than decisions made by compensatory schemes? In the abstract, most people say, "Yes, they *are* unreasonable. Noncompensation amounts to saying that one factor is infinitely more important than another, and that's ridiculous." For instance, it is easy to envision a loan applicant who fails to meet a collateral cut-off but has other strengths, such as an exceptionally good job, suggesting that the prospective loan is an outstanding credit risk. Regardless, the bank would have to reject the business.

Should you therefore discourage noncompensatory rules in your company? Not necessarily. Noncompensatory methods have their own strengths that make them sensible in certain situations. One strength is that they are easy to apply and to explain, which has implications for the acceptability issue. Compare, for example, MAUT to the loan rule sketched in this section. People are often less likely to argue about the details of a noncompensatory scheme than about, say, whether the weight assigned in MAUT to a particular consideration is too high or too low. Also, while noncompensatory schemes by design do not facilitate tradeoffs, they are indispensable in the early phases of a decision episode, when options are being screened and winnowed. For instance, job candidates who obviously fail to meet minimum physical requirements can be eliminated out of hand. Only later do the deciders *need* to make tradeoffs as they consider the surviving options.

So, in a given instance, should you encourage a compensatory or noncompensatory scheme? The answer should rest on a careful analysis—of the tradeoffs. A compensatory procedure that carefully trades off every strength of each option against every weakness should, in principle, result in the selection of the truly best alternative. But if the process takes a long time and if it causes lots of discord, the goodness of that best alternative might not make all the hassle worthwhile in the bigger scheme of things.

Deciders routinely face tradeoff problems distinct from the outcome × outcome tradeoffs considered so far. Although these problems cannot be addressed in depth here, some of the core ideas concerning outcome × outcome tradeoffs can be generalized to provide guidance on these problems, too. Here I will highlight a few aspects of other tradeoff situations where your judicious decision management efforts are likely to have especially useful impact.

Outcome × Uncertainty Tradeoffs

Imagine that your company must decide between two options: settle a lawsuit that has been filed against the company, or go to trial. The trial option offers a relatively good outcome for the company if the company wins the trial; the company would "only" have to pay $100,000 in legal fees. On the other hand, if the company loses the trial, it would have to pay an additional $1,000,000 beyond its legal fees. In contrast, the settle option requires an expenditure of $250,000, pure and simple.

This simplified scenario has the core elements of all outcome × uncertainty tradeoff problems. If your company were guaranteed to win the trial, then, obviously, going to trial would be the sensible alternative. But if a loss in court were assured, then settling would be the way to go. This is where the tradeoff concept enters the picture: There are no guarantees about what would in fact happen in court; the jury's verdict is an uncertain event. But the more *likely* it is that your company would win the trial, the more attractive should be the trial option. (Variations in the payoffs would have similar effects on the appeal of the alternatives. Thus, larger and larger potential judgments against your company would make the trial option less and less reasonable.) A good framing of the outcome × uncertainty tradeoff problem here is therefore this: "Just *how* likely must a win be in order to justify going to trial rather than settling?" All outcome × uncertainty tradeoff dilemmas have this spirit.

Significant elements of what is sometimes called "formal decision theory" are devoted to developing and justifying particular schemes for making outcome × uncertainty tradeoffs.[6] Some of those schemes involve what are called "mathematical expectations," for example, sums of potential payoffs, each weighted (that is, multiplied) by what is taken to be its probability. Others, with which you might well be more familiar, are embodied in the risk-versus-return rules common in finance.

Reducing Uncertainty

One simple way to have significant positive impact on how your company deals with outcome × uncertainty tradeoffs focuses on the uncertainty. Frequently, deciders are overly eager to apply the convenient schemes they have available for making those tradeoffs. In the legal decision problem, *someone* has to provide a judgment (however crude or precise) of your company's chances of winning in court. If things were to proceed the way I have seen so often, the deciders will get a single judgment from a single presumed expert (say, a 60 percent chance of winning). As discussed in connection with the judgment issue, the quality of the decision can be no better than that judgment's accuracy permits. The valuable service you can provide is simply reminding the deciders of this fact, not allowing them to be enticed into making outcome × uncertainty tradeoffs before exhausting their means for assuring accuracy. This would include applying the ideas of Chapter Six, for instance, acquiring the judgments of several independent, verified experts.

Challenging Attitudes Toward Risk

Picture two managers pondering the lawsuit decision. They hold identical beliefs about the company's chances of winning the trial. Yet, where one manager vigorously advises going to trial, the second equally strongly advocates settling. The reason is that they differ in their aversion to risk. Deciders' risk attitudes are normally taken as facts of life; they are unquestioned. The same is true in financial planning; planners usually start out by trying to determine a client's comfort level with risk, and they adjust their advice accordingly.

To a point, people's risk attitudes do indeed reflect fundamental, hard-to-change elements of their constitutions, their *personalities.*[7] The problem is that deciders' risk attitudes can lead to decisions that harm the company's interests. Some research suggests that this happens often. For instance, one classic study observed severe risk aversion in the investment decisions of a large corporation's executives.[8] The researcher suggested that the company would have been better served by riskier decisions whose long-run returns would have more than offset the occasional, easily absorbed losses those decisions would have yielded.

You would do well to persuade your company's deciders to challenge their risk attitudes when deciding on the company's behalf. For instance, in discussions about lawsuits against the company, the question to ask and answer is this: "What kind of risk attitude is likely to best serve the company's interests, and why?" The deciders would then proceed accordingly.

Outcome × Time Tradeoffs

Figure 7.4 shows the projected cash flows for a pair of small investment opportunities, each of which requires the same initial commitment. Thus, the Arthurs project promises $10,000 in Years 2 and 3 and $50,000 in Year 4, whereas the Henderson project is expected to yield $10,000 in Year 1, $20,000 in Year 2, $30,000 in Year 3, and nothing thereafter. This example illustrates the third major kind of tradeoff common in business, outcome × time tradeoffs. An essential feature of outcome × time tradeoffs is that

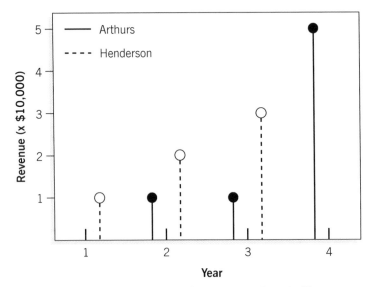

Figure 7.4. Cash Flow Diagram for Alternative Investment Opportunities

at least some consequences would be experienced at some distance in the future. And, typically, that distance matters. For instance, $10 today appeals more than a promise of $10 next week.

Standard business tools for making outcome × time tradeoffs rely on discounted cash flow concepts.[9] These include, for example, compounding formulas for computing present values. Applying a logic not unlike that of MAUT, discounted cash flow methods dictate that a company's deciders should select the available investment opportunity that has, for example, the best net present value. There are several points in the application of these methods where a decision manager can make substantial contributions, although I can only mention a couple.

Projections

The first contribution is constantly reminding company deciders that cash flow estimates are no more than that—estimates, that is, judgments. In the abstract, the deciders always realize this. But I have been struck by how often, once an analysis has been performed on projected cash flows, the conclusions are treated as gospel. The squishiness of their original foundations is pushed into the background, and confident, extreme decisions result. A reminder of the role of human judgment in the process should encourage badly needed skepticism and caution, in the spirit of the regressiveness principle. But it should also encourage the deciders to seek to improve the accuracy of projections, using the judgment ideas suggested in Chapter Six, for instance, synthesizing multiple judgments in particular ways.

Discounting

The second contribution concerns the discount rates deciders apply in making outcome × time tradeoffs. These are the rates by which, for instance, the company determines just how much money in hand right now ($800? $745? $670?) is considered

equivalent to $1,000 due two years hence. Numerous consider-
ations figure into deciders' reasoning when settling on the rate
applied in a given situation, including assessments of opportunity costs, inflation, risk, and impatience. And every company
has customs for how, exactly, to achieve a synthesis of these
considerations. Your contribution is promoting (if not leading)
a critical review of those customs: Exactly what *are* our customs? Where did they originate? Do they serve our interests?
How should we refine them?

Deciders' final tradeoffs normally signal the point where
they have decided: "This is what we're going to do." But the ultimate success or failure of the decision often hinges critically
on how particular parties feel about the decision and on the
execution of various plans, which are the subjects of the next
chapter.

CHAPTER SUMMARY

Probably the thing that makes decision making most distinctive and difficult as a variety of problem solving is the fact that different people can
hold markedly different values for the same decision outcomes. The value
issue entails an assessment of how key parties will in fact like and dislike
the potential outcomes of prospective actions. Some of the prescriptions
in this chapter can assist deciders in dealing with this difficult challenge
by improving the accuracy of valuation judgments. Others suggest ways
to cope with the factors that often suppress the predictability of people's
values.

Virtually every decision situation eventually reaches a point where
deciders face one or more types of tradeoffs. Every company already has
in place informal and formal customs for dealing with tradeoffs. As a decision manager, you can improve these customs by providing guidance
about coping with their vulnerable elements. Tables 7.1 and 7.2 summarize the principal recommendations in this chapter for managing both
cardinal decision issues.

Table 7.1. **Managing the Value Issue**

Key Value Issue Hazards and Challenges	Specific Recommendations
Overlooking parties whose values matter	Beneficiary and stakeholder inventories and checklists
False consensus	Presume false consensus; seek others' corroboration; role-play others' lives
Limited candor, self-insight	Complementary sources; questioning by neutral parties; simulations
Reliance on weak value indicators	Exploit regressiveness and cumulative validity principles
Misguided intuitions	Seek independent corroboration

Table 7.2. **Managing the Tradeoffs Issue**

Key Tradeoffs Issue Hazards and Challenges	Specific Recommendations
Outcome × Outcome Dilemmas	
■ Anxiety and disagreement	■ MAUT
■ Pain of sacrifice	■ Dominance striving, stimulated by MAUT
■ Economic importance misjudgment	■ Instruction in proper meaning of *importance;* framing as judgment; judgment accuracy enhancement methods
■ Personal importance misjudgment	■ Economic importance recom- mendations, adapted; beneficiary specification; value judgment recommendations
■ Appeal of noncompensatory schemes	■ Weigh ease, acceptability of noncompensation against sensible- ness of compensatory methods

Table 7.2. **Managing the Tradeoffs Issue, Cont'd**

Key Tradeoffs Issue Hazards and Challenges	Specific Recommendations
Outcome × Uncertainty Dilemmas	
■ Tradeoffs predicated on inaccurate judgments	■ Apply judgment accuracy methods *before* making tradeoffs
■ Tradeoffs based on improper risk attitudes	■ Challenge deciders' risk attitudes
Outcome × Time Dilemmas	
■ Tradeoffs predicated on inaccurate projections	■ Counsel caution; shore up accuracy
■ Tradeoffs guided by inappropriate discount rates	■ Critically review and refine discounting customs

Questions for Consideration

1. Bring to mind an instance from your own business experience when deciders in a company were so troubled by a tradeoff dilemma that it significantly affected their normal functioning. As a decision manager at a level in the company comparable to your present position, what measures could you take that would most substantially reduce the disruption wreaked by future tradeoff dilemmas?

2. Two important facts of decision life are that different people value the same things in different ways, and that most business decisions have several beneficiaries, not just one. Thus, if the deciders select one alternative, the outcomes will please some beneficiaries but displease others. Offer a good illustration of this dilemma in a significant decision problem you have seen in your company. How did the deciders address the dilemma? How would you improve on what they did?

Ensuring Smooth Sailing

The Acceptability and Implementation Issues

Sally Robertson, head of the Knowledge Management Project at the Cramer Company, was steamed. Robertson felt that her team members were making far too few contributions to the team's knowledge sharing database. So at the next meeting, she laid down the law: "From now on, everybody has to post five comments on the database every week—no exceptions." Expecting "the usual whining," Robertson refused to entertain discussion about this new requirement. After a couple of weeks, few team members were complying with Robertson's demand. And many of the comments that were posted had no substance. Example: "Had a meeting with Dave Burney. He is doing well." Water cooler commentary was discouraging, too, for instance: "When she dropped that one on us, I said to myself: 'Here we go again—another useless, time-consuming edict from the big boss on high.'"

Sometimes when people make a decision, they have a free hand to do as they wish and, once they have decided, the deed is done and they can move on. When Sally Robertson goes to get herself a cup of coffee at the shop down the street from her office, the choice of size and flavor is solely hers. She makes her decision, and moves on. Decisions like these can be contrasted to *constrained project decisions*, for which the actions of people besides the deciders are significant and the selected alternative entails a host of activities—a project—that must occur successfully in order to achieve the deciders' aims. Sally Robertson's knowledge sharing database decision was such a decision. It was not only her tastes that mattered: the opinions of the other people on her Knowledge Management Project (as well as those of other parties to the decision, including her bosses) had great significance. And after she decided to require five database contributions every week, her intended aim could be achieved only if her team members actually did the work.

Many if not most big decisions in business are constrained project decisions. Suppose that, for any particular decision problem, the deciders in your company have done well by the cardinal decision issues discussed so far. Often this warrants confidence that the resulting decision will be an effective one. Yet in the case of constrained project decisions, there is a good chance that the results will be no better than those Sally Robertson experienced. That is, the project will fall short, if it gets off the ground at all. The deciders will have tripped up on the acceptability and implementation issues.

■ The Acceptability Issue

Chapter One articulated the acceptability issue, Cardinal Decision Issue 9, in these terms:

> How can we get them to agree to this decision
> and this decision procedure?

The prototypical acceptability disaster goes something like this:

- *Phase 1: Decision.* The deciders make a decision.
- *Phase 2: Objection.* Another party—not necessarily publicly—objects to the decision or to how it was reached.
- *Phase 3: Trouble.* The displeasure of the objecting party motivates actions that create trouble for the decision's intended beneficiaries, thereby damaging the effectiveness of the decision.

The incident involving Sally Robertson's five-comment decision clearly fit the prototype. First, Robertson decided to establish her five-comment rule. Then the people on her Knowledge Management Project objected. Finally, as a result, they created problems for Robertson, for the project, and for the company; the decision failed.

Strategies for Averting Acceptability Disasters

You would do your company a great service if you prevented deciders from backing into acceptability disasters. How can you do that? It is useful to recognize that, when deciders have mishandled the acceptability issue, it is often because they have mishandled prior cardinal decision issues in particular ways. Sally Robertson's five-comment disaster plausibly was a direct consequence of her misjudging whether her team members would simply refuse to comply with her demand, a failing with respect to the judgment issue; she was already aware that they might be displeased with the demand (as indicated by her assumption that they would whine about it). One tack you can take is simply sensitizing deciders to the need to include consideration of potential objectors in their deliberations of decision problems, right from the start. That is, standard company practice would have deciders keep in mind the potential for serious objections when addressing the possibilities issue for any major decision.

Alternatively, or in addition, the company can establish the custom of applying the following "acceptability checklist strategy," especially for significant, high-stakes decisions:

- *Step 1: Tentative Decision.* The deciders reach a tentative decision using their normal procedures.
- *Step 2: Checklist Review.* The deciders review their tentative decision according to the "Acceptability Checklist" shown in Figure 8.1.
- *Step 3: Revision.* The deciders revise their tentative decision according to what the checklist review reveals.

Precisely what the acceptability checklist strategy involves depends on the decision problem at hand, and it draws heavily on the deciders' creativity. But it is the first item in the checklist, the Who question, that conditions the details most heavily.

- **Who:** Who are the potential objectors?

- **Why:** Why might the objectors object to the decision?

- **Risk:** How capable and willing are the objectors to create serious trouble for the beneficiaries if they are displeased with the decision?

- **Prevention:** What can we do to preclude the trouble if not the objections themselves?

Figure 8.1. Acceptability Checklist

Take another look at Figure 2.1, which depicts the usual parties to any business decision. That picture can serve as, in effect, a highly functional checklist. Recall that each decision party is actually a role; a single person can play several of the roles in the same decision episode. As far as acceptability is concerned, the focal role is that of stakeholder. When stakeholders are displeased, they become *objectors*. So, for example, the other members of Sally Robertson's Knowledge Management Project were stakeholders for her five-comment decision even though, as members of the team and the company staff, they were beneficiaries, too. As objecting stakeholders, they had enormous power and they used it to subvert Robertson's decision.

More generally, there are three classes of potentially objecting stakeholders the deciders in your company should seek out for any tentative decision: co-deciders, co-beneficiaries, and pure stakeholders. The next sections outline key ideas you should make sure your company's deciders keep in mind as they pursue the Why, Risk, and Prevention questions for each category of potential objectors.

Co-Deciders

Recall the discussion in Chapter Four about the mode issue, which largely concerns the question of who makes a particular decision. For nonroutine decisions especially, several people are authorized or required to be involved as co-deciders. Relationships among the co-deciders actually define two kinds of decision situations: collaborations and negotiations. In a collaboration, the deciders are *partners* with the common goal of reaching a decision that best serves the company's interests. Any committee in your company engages in such collaborations, for instance, the division's operating committee when choosing among cost-cutting proposals. In a negotiation, there are at least two distinct groups of co-deciders, which we could call *opposites*, who are attempting to serve parties whose interests are at least partly opposed. Before any decision can be finalized and enacted, all sides must agree. Labor negotiations are the classic example. But less formal discussions, such as those among design, engineering, and manufacturing departments about new product features, are negotiations, too.

Collaborations

Picture yourself as a decision collaborator, for instance, a member of your unit's promotion committee. Why might a fellow collaborator, Jess Burke, disagree with a promotion decision you favor and hence try to block it? Collaborators tend to have any or all of three major reasons for objecting to a partner's preferred decision: wisdom, process, and self-interest.

Objection 1: Wisdom. Objectors might honestly doubt that the decision advocated by a partner would serve commonly held interests. For instance, Jess Burke might have what feel like legitimate reasons to question the long-term potential of your favorite promotion candidate.

Wisdom objections are very common, especially when one partner has reservations about another's experience or expertise. An especially effective way to head off wisdom objections is collaborative deliberation. Even when a decider has preconceived notions about what ought to be done about a decision problem, it is smart to resist the temptation to offer that proposal immediately. It is better to encourage a truly participative discussion about the problem, full of requests such as, "So what do *you* think, Jess?" Any personally preferred option should be offered within the flow of that discussion. The main reason that collaborative deliberation reduces wisdom objections so effectively is that the participants develop a sense of ownership for any decision that emerges. Every participant then feels: "*I* made that decision." Research has shown that people are highly confident in the correctness of their own decisions.[1] Moreover, few of us publicly criticize and undermine our own decisions even when we privately question their good sense.

Objection 2: Process. Objectors sometimes dislike the process by which a partner's decision was (or is being) made. Jess Burke might (even if only privately) oppose your favored candidate because of a belief—correct or mistaken—that you are advocating for that candidate because of personal friendship, not merit.

As noted in Chapter Four in the discussion about the mode issue, people have surprisingly strong emotions about the right ways to decide, feelings that are often grounded in deeply ingrained cultural values. Witness, for instance, the alarms that go off in many people's heads in the United States when they perceive threats to "democratic principles," "the right to choose," and "fairness." Or consider the disdain held by many people in Japan for decision tools such as open debate and simple majority rule. When handled crudely, U.S.-style tools can threaten the "face" and social harmony so treasured in traditional Japanese culture. Note that in debate and majority rule, there are, virtually always and by design, winners and losers. How are the losers supposed to feel? What are they supposed to do to cope with their embarrassment? As also observed in Chapter Four, every company (indeed, every *person*) has, over time, evolved a host of decision-making customs. And the people in that company are typically skeptical when an outsider comes along and says, "Do it this new way," which is heard as, "You've been doing it all wrong, you rubes."

A simple, workable prescription for heading off process objections has two elements. The first is observation: watch and learn the preferred local decision customs and go with the flow, suggesting refinements within the basic framework provided by those customs. The second element is direct: ask co-deciders how they would like to decide, for instance, beginning a meeting with a request like: "So, how do you folks think we ought to proceed?" Then inject your own preferences (hopefully building on ideas from this book) within the context of the ensuing discussion.

Objection 3: Self-Interest. When deciders believe that a co-decider's preferred decision would harm their personal interests, it is virtually guaranteed that they will object, even though they will probably hide the true reasons for their objections. So, for example, Jess Burke might oppose your top candidate for promotion because of fears that, if promoted, that candidate would create problems for Burke's own office.

We tend to bemoan self-interest objections, attributing them to "company politics," which we think contaminate the company's decision processes and therefore ought to be stamped out. But this is unrealistic. As discussed earlier, human nature demands that all deciders see themselves as beneficiaries for the decision at hand, too. After all, only in extreme circumstances do people willingly take actions that are self-destructive.

One prescription for self-interest objections applies to those responsible for assembling decision groups, for instance, committees. If you are in that position, your goal should be to ensure that, collectively, the interests of the co-deciders are balanced. That is, there should be no single large contingent of co-deciders with common interests who could, if they wished, dictate the group's decisions in order to serve those interests. Ideally, you should seek to ensure that all major constituencies for the committee's decisions are represented, too. This requires, of course, research to discover what those interests are. Suppose you had had a say in assembling the promotion committee on which you and Jess Burke served. Ideally, you would have sought out the plausible significance of every potential promotion for the interests of every committee membership candidate.

One self-interest situation has special significance, that involving subordinates and superiors, decision agents and their principals. As far as the company is concerned, an authorized decider is the one responsible for a decision even if the actual making of that decision is commissioned to another. In a particular sense, then, a decision agent and the person who bestowed decision responsibility on the agent are co-deciders. Normally, such agents need not worry that a decision will be blocked. But they must be concerned about the implications of the principal's opinion of that decision. For instance, when production manager Hank Warren ponders replacing Press #8, he wisely asks himself about his boss, Gene Flowers: "What would Gene say and do if this didn't work out—or if it *did?*"

As suggested in the discussion in Chapter Four about decision agency, a serious hazard that you should pursue as a decision manager is the possibility that the company's deciders believe that it is in their personal interests to decide in ways that harm the company's interests. If the deciders hold those beliefs, they will no doubt decide in accord with those assumptions, and the company will suffer for it. Chapter Seven illustrated one instance of this problem, describing the tendency for executives of a large corporation to make company investments in a highly risk-averse fashion even though the company could easily absorb the occasional losses that more appropriate, less risk-averse investment strategies would yield. The same forces are thought to contribute to another well-studied phenomenon, the tendency for deciders to escalate their commitment to projects that they personally initiated when those projects are clearly failing. For instance, loan officers who make loans that are going sour are significantly less likely to write those loans off than are other officers who had nothing to do with awarding those loans.[2]

The common foundation of both excessive risk aversion and dysfunctional commitment to failing projects is deciders' fear of the harm that others—particularly their superiors—will inflict on them for making decisions that result in setbacks for the company. ("I'll get demoted—or fired!") This fear speaks to the importance of the decision quality concepts discussed in Chapter Two. You can do your company a big favor by helping to create a company consensus on practices for treating deciders whose decisions have negative outcomes. Consider the problem close to home. What would and should *you* do if a subordinate makes a decision that embarrasses you personally, leading your superiors to say things like, "Are you people *totally* incompetent?" If you are like most people, your natural inclination would be to discipline or perhaps even dismiss the subordinate. You would say to yourself, "Well, he won't do *that* again, will he?" That would be shortsighted.

The following routine, consistent with the ideas in Chapter Two, makes more sense in a situation where a subordinate's decision yields significant adverse results:

- *Step 1: Investigation and Learning.* Investigate why the calamity occurred, drawing on the spirit of causal factor analysis as discussed in Chapter Two. Ask: "Does this incident suggest a fundamental flaw in how we decide here, or was this simply an unavoidable chance occurrence?" Then: "What can we learn that would make our decision procedures even stronger in the future?"

- *Step 2: Process and Effort.* Determine the process by which the decider decided. Although no one can guarantee that every decision will be an effective one, it is essential that deciders be held accountable for diligently applying good decision procedures. So if, after careful study, you fairly conclude that your subordinate's ineffective decision was due to a failure to use good procedures because of ignorance, you would take him aside and say something like: "Let me show you . . . " And if you discover that the culprit was laziness, you would be foolish to do anything other than make it clear to your subordinate and everyone else that a lack of diligence will not be tolerated.

Negotiations

The knee-jerk reaction of many negotiators is to object to every proposal by their opposites, under the assumption that the parties' interests are diametrically opposed. ("If those guys are proposing it, it has to be a bad deal for us!") As noted in the earlier discussion of negotiations in Chapter Five, contemporary negotiation experts widely recognize that most negotiation situations are quite different from this zero-sum expectation.[3] That is, the interests of the parties conflict only partly. Therefore, negotiations are more fruitfully framed as collaborative efforts to create settlements that improve the circumstances of both parties. As a decision manager, you can encourage company-wide acceptance of that view. Then, when people in the company approach any negotiation, they would be less likely to uncritically object to every proposal from the other side, and this stance is likely to be reciprocated eventually, at least to a point.

Co-Beneficiaries

Co-beneficiaries are distinct categories of people whose interests a decision is meant to serve. Often, however, the interests of co-beneficiaries are at least partly in opposition. Imagine, for example, that your company is considering a proposal that would improve customer service by extending hours. This action would indeed make things better for customers who are inconvenienced by your current hours. But to pay for this improvement, your company must increase prices a bit, a burden that must be shared by all customers, even those who do not take advantage of the extended service. This new service would also make life a little harder for those company employees compelled to work at times that they would prefer to be at home. To the extent that the company sees its employees as beneficiaries of its policies, the proposed decision would damage their interests.

Co-beneficiaries who are harmed by a decision will naturally object and, if they can, take actions that hurt the company. For instance, at least some of the customers who derive no benefit from your extended hours but must nevertheless pay for them will drift to your competitors. And the disgruntled employees required to work inconvenient hours will be less cooperative in their work generally. Again, the full acceptability checklist strategy needs to be applied to deal with co-beneficiary conflicts, with a special emphasis on the Who question. That is because it is easy for deciders to forget important co-beneficiaries when trying to serve the interests of the beneficiaries who have claimed their attention at the moment. It would not be surprising, for example, if the executives who make the extended hours decision are simply oblivious to customers and workers who might take exception to their decision.

Extensions of two ideas you have seen before can provide guidance for devising effective ways of dealing with the objections of co-beneficiaries. The first idea entails tradeoffs. To the degree that different co-beneficiaries' interests are in opposition, it will be impossible for the company to please all co-beneficiaries. So, applying the concepts of Chapter Seven, the company's deciders must deliberately seek to determine the true relative importance of serving and failing to serve the competing interests of the various co-beneficiaries. If such an exercise supports the conclusion that the interests of other customers and employees outweigh those of customers who would welcome extended hours, then the proposal to extend hours at your company should be rejected. The second useful idea is to generalize the spirit of contemporary *integrative negotiation* practices. In this context, this perspective would encourage deciders to recognize that the interests of co-beneficiaries that appear to be in pure, direct opposition probably are not that way in reality. Specifically, different groups of co-beneficiaries are likely to have needs and tastes that are quite distinct and can be, in essence, traded at little or no net loss to the company. For example, it might easily be possible to offer inexpensive yet attractive privileges to employees willing to work at the unpopular times the company's extended service hours would require.

Pure Stakeholders

The pure stakeholder role involves nondeciders and nonbeneficiaries whose actions can affect the interests of a decision's beneficiaries. Two quite different kinds of pure stakeholders are important to distinguish, petitioners and nonpetitioners.

Petitioners
Petitioners are parties who make specific requests and must await decisions from your company in response to their requests. Some of the most important petitioners include employees proposing new projects, products, procedures, or policies; potential customers requesting bids on products they need; vendors asking the company to buy their products; and other companies suggesting joint ventures or mergers. Petitioners obviously object when the company decides to reject their petitions. But what is most problematic—the most serious Why—is not the rejections as such, because, as every sales representative realizes, companies *must* reject more petitions than they grant. Where companies get in trouble is with *how* they say no. Ungracious or insulting refusals—including unexplained refusals—enrage petitioners and ignite a determination to retaliate.

The clear prescription is to invest in the development of skills and customs for saying no gracefully and informatively. Company deciders who must say no need a well-thought-out protocol for doing so that is respectful and tells petitioners how their petitions fall short, to the extent that this is not competitively or legally compromising. Most petitioners will recognize that they have learned something useful and, in due course, the company itself might well benefit from that learning. Although this prescription is undeniably expensive, it is a legitimate business expense that pays off in the long run.

Nonpetitioners
The aims a company's deciders are trying to achieve typically have nothing to do with nonpetitioning stakeholders, such as the residents in neighborhoods surrounding your company's facilities. That is why nonpetitioners are so easy to overlook, leading to nasty surprises such as the protests that catch companies off guard. Some years ago, for instance, several insurance companies decided to stop writing insurance policies for women who were victims of battering.[4] As far as the companies were concerned, the women were poor actuarial risks, and denying them policies was a sound business decision that served the interests of their shareholders. The companies seem to have been blindsided by the outrage expressed by members of Congress and by advocacy groups.

Because nonpetitioning objectors can materialize seemingly magically from any direction, there is clearly a premium on the Who and Why questions in the acceptability checklist strategy. That is, the biggest challenge is identifying the people who are probable objectors to a decision and what would bother them about that decision. Once these parties have been thoroughly inventoried, the task of crafting measures for dealing with their objections follows the principles discussed earlier.

Who-why exercises are an effective tool for identifying potential nonpetitioning objectors and their objections. The technique is an adaptation of tools such as brainstorming and the nominal group technique (Chapter Five), which exploit the collective coverage advantage of groups. So, for example, after the deciders in your company have reached a tentative decision, they might convene several groups of broadly chosen participants and give them this charge: "This is what we are thinking of doing, and this is how we got here. . . . Who, if anyone, do you think might have a problem with this—and why?" The format is profitably extended through outright role-playing, with an improvisation prompt like this one: "Now, you are an ambitious, muck-raking reporter for the morning paper. You have just learned about this decision from a trusted source. Dictate what you will say in the most scathing critical article you can write about it."

■ The Implementation Issue

In Chapter One, the implementation issue, Cardinal Decision Issue 10, was expressed as follows:

> That's what we decided to do. Now, how can we
> get it done, or *can* we get it done, after all?

Sally Robertson's decision to require five weekly entries into her Knowledge Management Project database clearly foundered on this issue, too. The decision was never actually implemented because her team members refused to cooperate or perhaps because it was impossible for them to do what she commanded.

As suggested by Sally Robertson's experience, the implementation issue is different from the earlier cardinal decision issues in that it is a derivative of them. That is, to the extent that deciders do badly by the implementation issue, it is because they have done badly by particular instances of prior issues.

Acceptability Issue Origins

Problems with the acceptability issue are often the main culprit. As in the Sally Robertson case, various stakeholders must carry out the projects initiated by many business decisions. Those people might drag their feet if not sabotage the projects outright if they disagree with the decisions initiating them. Acceptability measures such as those discussed earlier in this chapter obviously reduce the hazard of implementation problems as well.

Adaptations of Japanese *nemawashi* practices are advisable, too.[5] *Nemawashi* is the custom whereby, when a proposal for a major company activity arises, a person we might call a "decision shepherd" is designated. In a series of private, off-line meetings, the shepherd thoroughly discusses the proposal with *every* key party whose actions could eventually affect the proposal's implementation. The goal is to reach consensus—unanimous, not majority, agreement—among all these parties. Naturally, this requires negotiating refinements along the way, such that, at the end, the proposal might bear little resemblance to what it looked like at the beginning, if it survives the process at all. Making decisions via *nemawashi* takes a long time by U.S. standards. But many Japanese managers would argue that this extra time is more than offset by the resulting ease of implementation. After all, there is greater buy-in by all the key players, and the process surfaces all kinds of impediments the deciders would overlook otherwise.

Possibilities, Judgment, and Options Issues Foundations

Managers sometimes say things like this: "Our decision was perfectly fine. It's just the execution that was a disaster." Do not allow the deciders in your company to fall into the trap this line of thinking represents, for there is a sensible rejoinder to it:

> It was a disaster, all right. But when you decided to approve the project, why didn't you anticipate the factors that made the project fail? You could then have planned better, thereby making failure unlikely. Or else you would have recognized that the chances of success were slim and therefore rejected the project as unfeasible.

The rejoinder implicates the role of the possibilities and judgment issues in many cases of poor implementation. Lots of failed projects are undertaken because of overly optimistic forecasts of things like task completion times. These are often described as instances of the "planning fallacy," a pervasive tendency to believe that we will finish tasks in less time than they will actually take.[6] One basis for these overly sanguine predictions is a variety of oversight closely akin to those involved in problems with the possibilities issue generally. When deciders formulate their forecasts, they tend to rely especially heavily on a mental walk-through of the process by which the project would be carried out. Research suggests that such walk-throughs often neglect the obstacles that real life is apt to erect along the way. The measures for assuring adequate resolution of the possibilities and judgment issues discussed in Chapter Six and applied to prospective project outcomes can significantly reduce the odds of undertaking doomed projects.

All too often, when deciders approve a project, what they are really approving are only the *aims* of the project. This seems to have been the case at a company I will call AgriSyn after it acquired another company, Ecosure. A project intended to integrate the companies' information technology systems was a high-priced disaster. My educated guess is that the AgriSyn management board felt that it was a no-brainer that there should be an effort to integrate the two IT systems. They then gave far less thought than they should have to the details. ("Just get on with it," they thought—or even said—but the two systems were in fact incompatible at a level that made it exceptionally hard to merge them.) This illustrates how failing to adequately resolve the options and possibilities issues wreaks havoc with implementation.

When you see deciders in your company pondering projects, try to persuade them to devote more attention than seems necessary to the particulars of achieving the worthy aims of those projects. The challenge is creating solid options for implementation plans. The following are among the most frequent omissions from such plans:

- *Champions:* Many projects die short of their aims because no one with weight in the company was assigned the responsibility of seeing the projects through.
- *Incentives:* Other projects wither because the people whose efforts are required to make them succeed are preoccupied with other, more high-priority duties in the company; they are given no incentives to make the projects work.
- *Resources:* Many other projects fall by the wayside because they are undersupported with respect to required resources generally.

Urge the deciders to not sign off on a new project unless and until they see convincing evidence that the plans for carrying the project through have good odds of succeeding. Plans should be revised until they can survive this scrutiny. Recall that this is the spirit of the O-P-O cycles technique for option refinement discussed in Chapter Six.

Your tour of core decision management ideas is complete. You are now well positioned to begin assuring that every organization you touch in your company decides better because you were there, and that everyone recognizes your contributions. Some ideas about how you can begin and sustain this impact are the subject of the next and final chapter.

CHAPTER SUMMARY

Company decisions are typically subject to all manner of threats that key parties will object. Before signing off on any decision, deciders are well advised to take a variety of specific measures for exploring the acceptability of both their decision and their decision process with a view to reducing those threats. It is also commonplace for major business decisions to fail in the implementation phase. Most implementation disasters are traceable to deciders' mishandling of particular elements of the processes by which the decisions initiating the projects were made. Tables 8.1 and 8.2 summarize actions deciders can take to reduce the odds of such errors with respect to the acceptability and implementation issues.

Table 8.1. Managing the Acceptability Issue

Key Acceptability Issue Hazards and Challenges	Specific Recommendations
Obliviousness to stakeholders' potential objections	Acceptability checklist strategy—the Who, Why, Risk questions
Inadequate objection prevention	
▪ Co-deciders: collaborations	▪ Collaborative deliberations; process preference accommodation; decider self-interest management, including failure responding
▪ Co-deciders: negotiations	▪ Framing as collaborative, mutually beneficial settlement creation
▪ Co-beneficiaries	▪ Deliberate discernment of relative importance to company interests; integrative negotiations among co-beneficiaries
▪ Pure stakeholders: petitioners	▪ Customs for graceful, respectful, informative rejections
▪ Pure stakeholders: nonpetitioners	▪ Who-why exercises

Table 8.2. Managing the Implementation Issue

Key Implementation Issue Hazards and Challenges	Specific Recommendations
Stakeholder noncooperation, interference	Acceptability issue measures; *nemawashi* adaptations
Plan impediment oversights, misjudgment (including planning fallacy)	Possibilities and judgment issue methods, applied to implementation plans
Flawed implementation plans	
▪ Option generation taken lightly	▪ Option issue techniques, applied to plans
▪ Deficient implementation plans	▪ Possibilities issue methods, especially O-P-O cycles, applied to plans; plan essentials checklist: champions, incentives, resources

Questions for Consideration

1. What are the most serious instances you can recall personally where a company did badly by the acceptability and implementation issues, respectively? In terms of specifics about the company's decision customs, how would you explain *why* the company's deciders tripped up in those incidents? Suppose that only a single decision custom could be changed in the company. If your aim were to reduce the odds of similar acceptability and implementation mishaps in the future, what particular change would you promote, and why?

2. Top management at Oak Bank felt that, in order to keep ahead of the competition, they needed to sharply improve client services and attract lots of new clients. The plan for doing this was to assign each vice president or senior vice president to either of two separate roles: senior client manager or senior debt manager. The client managers were to spend most of their time out of the office with clients. The debt managers were to remain in the office analyzing proposed deals and executing transactions. Shortly after the plan was put in place, serious, unforeseen problems developed. Most notably, the bank was unable to handle the increased flow of deals. What would you expect to have been among the significant contributors to the problems with the reorganization plan? What might the Oak Bank leadership have done differently to avoid those difficulties?

3. Joe Strong, president of Purechem, was torn when Mark Lincoln, his controller, threatened to quit. Lincoln was a prized company asset. But at the moment, Purechem could ill afford a hefty salary hike, which Strong simply assumed it would take to keep Lincoln. After all, that is what *Strong* would have demanded. So negotiations never actually got off the ground, and Lincoln left. Strong later learned through the grapevine that what Lincoln really wanted was more prestige, not more money. Strong was flabbergasted: "A better title was no problem. That's free! Why didn't he just *tell* me?" Purechem lost out because Strong misjudged Lincoln's values for possible deals, a not uncommon error by opposites in negotiations. Reflect on negotiations you have observed in your own company. What do those observations (and Chapter Seven) suggest as effective ways your company could avoid such misjudgments and thereby achieve more mutually acceptable negotiated settlements?

Starting and Sustaining Decision Management Improvement Efforts

Ben: Carl, good to see you again! I was doing some work over here at Alliance and thought I'd just pop in and say hello.

Carl: Great to see you again, too, Ben!

Ben: So, Carl, the last time we talked was about a year ago, at the end of my exec ed course on decision making. You were fired up about putting into action a slew of the ideas we discussed. So tell me, how are they working out?

Carl: Well, gee, Ben, I'm kind of embarrassed to even talk about it. You know, when I got back here, it was like I had returned from a revival meeting, and I was just raring to go. And for a while, I really did try the ideas out. But it was a lot harder than I thought it would be. And, somehow, over time, I just got so bogged down putting out all the fires we get around here that, frankly, all the new decision ideas got lost in the shuffle. So I have to confess that not much—if any-thing—has really changed.

Ben: Oh, I see . . .

The Ben and Carl story is replayed thousands of times every week, in every context where people learn a new set of in-sights or methods and then seek to apply them in their everyday situations. Whether the concern is corporate strategy or aerobic exercise, it seems to be the rule rather than the excep-tion that vows to follow through come to naught.

I expect that, having gotten this far in this book, you are now convinced that how well or poorly a company fares in the marketplace rests squarely on how well the people in the com-pany decide; you have seen this truth documented in one illus-tration after another. I suspect that you have also been persuaded that the quality of decision making in a company is not an acci-dent; it is a direct consequence of the leaders' decision manage-ment actions, whether deliberate or inadvertent. So you should be eager to get started on becoming (and profiting from becom-ing) a stellar decision manager. But the Ben and Carl story (and countless others like it) stirs great pessimism. There is every rea-son to anticipate that your resolve will erode and that backslid-ing will take over. So let me close with some ideas for how to keep that from happening.

■ Contributors to Backsliding

Why are we all subject to backsliding? There are five major culprits:

- *Urgency:* Often new efforts get lost in the urgency of every-day events—crises—that simply *have* to be dealt with right then and there: "There was just never a convenient time to try out the ideas. Everybody—me, especially, it seems—was overworked as it was, dealing with all the budget cuts and reorganizations that seem to be a way of life around here."

- *Forgetting:* The forgetting culprit is especially powerful because it rules out even the possibility of new ideas being used—once they are lost from memory, it is as if they never existed: "For the first couple of weeks, I thought about decision management stuff all the time. Eventually, after being away from them for so long, it rarely occurred to me to apply the new techniques, and when it did, I couldn't remember how things were supposed to go."

- *Hassle:* The heart of the hassle factor is that the desired change program fails because it demands out-of-the-ordinary efforts that are unsustainable over the long run: "To apply these concepts, I had to go out of my way, doing extra things that were on top of all the *other* things I was obliged to do and was in the habit of doing. I just didn't have the energy and willpower to keep that up."

- *Isolation:* The isolation factor reflects the powerful influence of social forces in virtually every aspect of our lives: "I was out there all by myself, a Lone Ranger. Most of the folks in my unit—and, even worse, my boss—thought I was nuts. They didn't understand what I was trying to do. And although they didn't actively fight it, they sure didn't try to help me out, either. I couldn't continue trying to march against the tide."

- *Incentives:* Any change effort is easily undermined by the apparent absence of immediate rewards for success: "After a couple of weeks, I couldn't honestly say that even my own decisions were making a dramatic difference in how well things were going in my work. And I certainly don't think that my boss was dazzled by spectacularly better decisions in our office. So I said, 'What's the point?'"

To avoid adding your own decision management experiences to the legions of Ben and Carl stories, you must somehow defeat every one of these demons. Doing so requires that you—*personally*—devise, adhere to, and continuously refine a plan that will ensure that you follow through, a plan that directly addresses each of the main contributors to backsliding.

■ Elements of a Successful Action Plan

If you develop your plan yourself, you will have the sense of personal ownership success demands. Moreover, the plan will be tailored to the unique circumstances of your personal situation and the situation in your company. Nevertheless, experience has demonstrated the wisdom of weaving a limited set of elements into a decision management action plan, elements that fall into just two broad categories: partnership and institutions.

Partnership

As noted back in Chapter One, you need partners—allies—in your decision management mission. Acquiring partners helps most directly with isolation and incentives. With partners, you will no longer be the sole voice for change. And when you and your partners achieve even subtle successes, at minimum you will be rewarded by your mutual congratulations. Just as important, though, you and your partners will be able to work collaboratively to put into place and sustain measures that combat all the remaining contributors to backsliding.

What kinds of partners should you seek to recruit? Although you should never turn away anyone in the company, it makes sense to start by seeking partnerships with a few close peers, managers at your own rank. You probably already know these folks well, including how they think. And you can empathize with the kinds of problems that occupy their attention day in and day out. Thus you have a natural bond on which you can build. Collectively, all of you should be motivated to craft measures that speak directly to the decision management ills that make your jobs harder than they ought to be and that are impeding your advancement. After getting things going, you and your peer collaborators would be wise to seek partners in the ranks above you, starting with your own bosses. After all, those are the people who control the richer resources and authority required for broad change.

How should you approach the recruiting task? The same principles that guide effective sales practices apply here, too. A prospective partner's self-perceived needs have special importance. Start by asking yourself, "What keeps this person up at night? What company problems cause the biggest worries? What does this person see as obstacles to personal advancement?" Using the kinds of ideas discussed in this book, figure out how and to what extent those problems arguably are caused or aggravated by weak decision management. Then make those arguments to your prospective partner as convincingly as you can. Experience has shown that you must illustrate your arguments with concrete, easy-to-understand horror stories from real-life business situations, such as those that are recounted in the news every day or, better still, that you can cite from the everyday life of your own company. To close the sale, offer a way out: improved decision management practices. ("Here are some things people like us have used to make a real difference.")

Institutions

The first order of business for you and your partners should be working to see that, gradually, new institutions are put into place, starting with your own work groups. By *institutions* I mean simply the customs, routines, and even tools that people in the company must apply in the everyday, run-of-the-mill conduct of their duties—what is considered normal. Making a decision management measure into an institution prevents backsliding because then people do not have to do anything extra or unusual. In fact, going *against* an institution is what is burdensome and therefore unlikely to occur. Here are five specific institutions to ponder.

Commitment

The company (or unit), in the persons of the official and unofficial influence leaders, makes a public commitment to the ideal of constantly improving decision management practices. It goes a long way for a supervisory committee to publicly say something like: "Our goal is to continuously and measurably improve how we make decisions in this division, top to bottom."

The only way such a commitment will ever occur is through the advocacy of high-level managers you have previously recruited as collaborators in your decision management efforts. They must make the same kinds of sales efforts you used to recruit *them*. Simply put, they must persuade the company's leadership that better decision management will significantly improve the company's performance, and hence the *leadership's* performance.

Czar

The leadership should appoint and publicly announce a point person or *czar* for monitoring and sustaining decision management improvement efforts. Moreover, the decision management czar must have the resources, in terms of both money and personnel, required for doing the job. It is important that the role of czar be only part of the portfolio of responsibilities for the person so appointed. Otherwise, it is unlikely that the role will ever be realized. ("The last thing we need around here is another position.") Moreover, in isolation, the role could easily be marginalized. Thus czar duties should be one of several acknowledged responsibilities of a high-level manager (such as a production manager or controller) who is already respected for other reasons. Critically, the company's improvements in decision management must have direct and significant impact on the czar's compensation.

Decision Management Brownbags

Long ago, the DuPont Company (where I worked for a while) transformed itself into a company with an outstanding safety culture. Every single person in this chemical giant, it seems, naturally views any situation that arises in terms of its safety implications. In their heads, questions like these just pop up spontaneously: "Is this dangerous? How can we make it safe?"

A key element of DuPont's remarkable ability to sustain this culture for decades is simple: every small work group in the company (even accounting and personnel selection research groups, like those to which I belonged) devotes perhaps fifteen to thirty minutes of a weekly brownbag lunch meeting to a conversation about safety. One member of the group is responsible for having done research or other preparation on some safety-significant topic. That member then presents the resulting findings and ideas and leads a lively discussion about them. Every member of the group, with no exceptions, is part of a regularly scheduled rotation of safety discussion leaders.

The DuPont cultural transformation and maintenance strategy is directly generalizable to decision management. With the requisite leadership support, you and your partners would initiate a tradition of periodic brief decision management brownbag discussions in company work groups modeled on the DuPont tradition. Just as safety consciousness has become second nature for everyone at DuPont, decision consciousness will become second nature at your company. This cultural makeover probably would have greater impact than any other single thing you could do to advance the cause of better decision making in the company.

Where would brownbag discussion leaders find their material? Reading and their own imaginations. The management practitioner literature, including publications such as *Harvard Business Review, Sloan Management Review,* and *Academy of Management Executive,* often has articles that speak more or less directly to the kinds of decision management problems that managers face, even if they do not use the expression "decision management." But decision-significant occurrences and ideas are everywhere. Even business and everyday newspapers prove to be a rich source of inspiration and material for any discussion leader. All these sources are wonderful tools for continuing one's personal development as a decision manager, too.

Decision Audits

The average person in any population is likely to be in decent if not especially good health. But cumulatively, as in the case of widespread obesity or hypertension, multitudes of apparently minor health problems add up to big problems for a society as a whole. Moreover, a serious disease that occurs only once in a blue moon is nevertheless catastrophic for the specific individual afflicted by it. And some rare illnesses, if sufficiently virulent and contagious, can precipitate society-wide disasters. Public health programs, neglected as they are, are worth their weight in gold because they avert these insidious robbers of a society's vitality.

It is useful to view a company's decision making as analogous to public health. The typical company decision is OK, if not great. Cumulatively, though, the minor shortcomings of thousands of little decisions—their discrepancies from greatness—add up and even compound one another's effects, gradually sapping the company's ability to compete. Further, if fundamental flaws in the company's decision practices remain hidden beneath the surface of everyday decisions, then the company is prey to occasional decision disasters whose catastrophic consequences cascade throughout the company. Decision management institutions are a company's decision-making health system, its means for preventing disasters and for assuring that even the average decision is an effective, healthy one.

Epidemics are obvious signals that something is badly amiss in the public's health and thus something drastic needs to be done. But low-key, quiet diseases (for example, asthma) often have greater impact on a society than some highly publicized epidemics. A public health system must therefore have regular, reliable means for monitoring the need for actions against such nondramatic threats, means such as periodic inspections and surveys. Similarly, spectacular, high-profile failed decisions, like Arthur Andersen's signing off on Enron's books, provide clear evidence that something is seriously wrong in a company's decision practices. And all such cases should be pursued using the causal factor analysis (CFA) methods sketched in Chapter Two. Yet to assure fundamental soundness of the company's decision making and therefore preclude spectacular failures, there need to be analogs to public health inspections and surveys. Decision audits should be institutionalized to serve that purpose.

The decision auditing idea is completely analogous to the notion of financial auditing. Accountants randomly sample and appraise transactions for indications of problems with a company's financial controls. Similarly, decision auditing entails periodically sampling company decisions in particular classes, for instance, supplier choices, major hires, or investment selections. The audit procedure would require an analysis and appraisal of the process by which each sampled decision was made, using the principles described throughout this book. ("How was the possibilities issue dealt with here? Was that good enough, considering the circumstances? What would have worked better?") Ideally, the findings would be uneventful; you would learn that every cardinal decision issue was handled well. But the results might also reveal weaknesses that, in due course, would spell serious trouble for the company. Clearly, in instances like that, the company's managers must act.

Decision audits serve another vital purpose, too. All the decision audits that have been performed in a given period, say, a year or half year, should be summarized. The resulting summaries provide visible yardsticks of the company's decision-making health. They also provide the proof you and your partners need to validate your efforts to yourselves and everyone else, allowing you to say: "See how much better we've gotten?"

Performance Appraisals and Compensation

The final suggested institution is actually a *requirement* for long-term success. You and your decision management partners should work hard to see that a regular element of the system by which managers' performance is appraised and, in turn, the managers are compensated, is how well they have carried out their decision management duties: directly influencing key decisions, supervising decision-making routines, shaping decision-making practices, and providing required decision-making resources. If the recognition and compensation that managers command is tied directly to these activities, they will do whatever it takes to do them well.

CHAPTER SUMMARY

Change efforts are notoriously subject to backsliding, and efforts to improve decision making in your company are no exception. A plan to ensure that your efforts are sustained needs to be personal and creative, and it must address the main contributors to backsliding. Two types of elements that should go into the plan are partnerships and new institutions. Five key institutions are commitment, a czar, decision management brownbags, regular decision audits, and appropriate use of performance appraisals and compensation.

Suppose you were to enact even *some* of the ideas discussed here. Then if I were to speak with you a year from now, our encounter would be much different from the one between Ben and Carl that opened this chapter. You would be well on your way to becoming (and remaining) a stellar decision manager, and so would everyone around you. Make it happen.

Questions for Consideration

1. Consider all the managers in your company you know personally. Which one would you try to recruit as your first ally in your efforts to improve decision management practices in the company? What makes that person such an attractive candidate? Sketch the approach you would use in your recruiting efforts, taking into account what you know that person finds important and persuasive.

2. Reflect on the key institutions discussed in this chapter: public company commitment to constantly improving decision management, appointment of a high-level decision management czar, decision management brownbags, decision auditing, and decision management effectiveness as a consideration in performance appraisals and compensation. Which of these institutions would be the first one you would work toward establishing in your company, starting in your own office—and why? What would be the key elements in your plan for building that institution? What makes those particular features so critical?

Notes

Chapter One

1. John Gallagher, "CEO Costs Borders $4 Million," *Detroit Free Press* (May 21, 1999): 1D-2D.
2. Thomas Grubb and Robert Lamb, "What Went Wrong at DCX?" *Detroit Free Press* (February 6, 2001): 7A.
3. Gallagher, "CEO Costs Borders $4 Million."

Chapter Two

1. *The Analects Attributed to Confucius* (James Legge translation), Chapter 13. Available online: http://www.4literature.net/Confucius/ Analects/13.html. Access date: July 19, 2002.
2. *Root Cause Analysis Handbook: A Guide to Effective Incident Investigation* (Knoxville, TN: EQE International, 1999).

Chapter Three

1. Julie Flaherty, "Suggestions Rise from the Floors of U.S. Factories," *New York Times* (April 18, 2001): C1, C7.
2. Kathleen M. Eisenhardt, "Strategy as Strategic Decision Making," *Sloan Management Review* 40, no. 3 (1999): 65–72.

3. Amos Tversky and Daniel Kahneman, "Belief in the 'Law of Small Numbers,'" *Psychological Bulletin* 76 (1971): 105–110.

4. Brad M. Barber and Terrance Odean, "Trading Is Hazardous to Your Wealth: The Common Stock Investment Performance of Individual Investors," *Journal of Finance* 55 (2000): 773–806.

Chapter Four

1. Charles F. Gettys, Rebecca M. Pliske, Carol Manning, and Jeff T. Casey, "An Evaluation of Human Act Generation Performance," *Organizational Behavior & Human Decision Processes* 39 (1987): 23–51.

2. Caryn Christensen, James R. Larson Jr., Ann Abbott, Anthony Ardolino, Timothy Franz, and Carol Pfeiffer, "Decision Making of Clinical Teams: Communication Patterns and Diagnostic Error," *Medical Decision Making* 20 (2000): 45–50.

3. Herbert H. Blumberg, "Group Decision Making and Choice Shift," in *Small Group Research: A Handbook,* edited by Alexander P. Hare, Herbert H. Blumberg, Martin F. Davies, and M. Valerie Kent (Stamford, CT: Ablex, 1994): pp. 195–210.

4. An example: J. Frank Yates and Ju-Whei Lee, "Chinese Decision Making," in *Handbook of Chinese Psychology,* edited by Michael H. Bond (Hong Kong: Oxford University Press, 1996): pp. 338–351.

5. J. Frank Yates, Paul C. Price, Ju-Whei Lee, and James Ramirez, "Good Probabilistic Forecasters: The 'Consumer's' Perspective," *International Journal of Forecasting* 12 (1996): 41–56.

6. Suzanne C. Kobasa, Salvatore R. Maddi, and Stephen Kahn, "Hardiness and Health: A Prospective Study," *Journal of Personality and Social Psychology* 42 (1982): 168–177.

Chapter Five

1. Leigh Thompson, *The Mind and Heart of the Negotiator* (Upper Saddle River, NJ: Prentice Hall, 1998).

2. Matt Richtel, "Online Revolution's Latest Twist: Computers Screening Job Seekers," *New York Times* (February 6, 2000): 1, 19.

3. R. Brent Gallupe and William H. Cooper, "Brainstorming Electronically," *Sloan Management Review* 35, no. 1 (1993): 27–36.

4. Alice M. Isen, Kimberly A. Daubman, and Gary P. Nowicki, "Positive Affect Facilitates Creative Problem Solving," *Journal of Personality and Social Psychology* 52 (1987): 1122–1131.

5. Kathleen M. Eisenhardt, "Speed and Strategic Choice: How Managers Accelerate Decision Making," *California Management Review* 32, no. 3 (1990): 39–54.

Chapter Six

1. John E. Hunter and Ronda F. Hunter, "Validity and Utility of Alternative Predictors of Job Performance," *Psychological Bulletin* 96 (1984): 72–98.

2. Richaurd Camp, Mary E. Vielhaber, and Jack L. Simonetti, *Strategic Interviewing* (San Francisco: Jossey-Bass, 2001).

3. J. Frank Yates, Roberta L. Klatzky, and Carolynn A. Young, "Cognitive Performance Under Stress," in *Emerging Needs and Opportunities for Human Factors Research,* edited by Raymond S. Nickerson (Washington, DC: National Academy Press, 1995): pp. 262–290.

4. Suzanne C. Kobasa, "Stressful Life Events, Personality, and Health: An Inquiry into Hardiness," *Journal of Personality & Social Psychology* 37 (1979): 1–11.

5. J. Scott Armstrong and P. D. Hutcherson, "Predicting the Outcome of Marketing Negotiations," *International Journal of Research in Marketing* 6 (1989): 227–239.

6. J. Frank Yates, Paul C. Price, Ju-Whei Lee, and James Ramirez, "Good Probabilistic Forecasters: The 'Consumer's' Perspective," *International Journal of Forecasting* 12 (1996): 41–56.

7. J. Frank Yates, "Subjective Probability Accuracy Analysis," in *Subjective Probability,* edited by George Wright and Peter Ayton (Chichester, England: Wiley, 1994): pp. 381–410.

8. J. Frank Yates, *Judgment and Decision Making* (Upper Saddle River, NJ: Prentice Hall, 1990). (See Chapter 8 in particular.)

9. P. B. Snow, D. S. Smith, and W. J. Catalona, "Artificial Neural Networks in the Diagnosis and Prognosis of Prostate Cancer: A Pilot

Study," *Journal of Urology,* 152 (1994): 1923–1926. Also: "Computers Outperform Doctors at Diagnosis," *Detroit Free Press* (January 3, 1995): 4D.

Chapter Seven

1. Gary Marks and Norman Miller, "Ten Years of Research on the False-Consensus Effect: An Empirical and Theoretical Review," *Psychological Bulletin* 102 (1987): 72–90.
2. Patricia B. Seybold, "Get Inside the Lives of Your Customers," *Harvard Business Review* 79, no. 5 (2001): 81–89.
3. Robert B. Zajonc, "Feeling and Thinking: Closing the Debate Over the Independence of Affect," in *Feeling and Thinking: The Role of Affect in Social Cognition,* edited by Joseph P. Forgas (New York: Cambridge University Press, 2000): pp. 31–58.
4. Leaf Van Boven, David Dunning, and George Loewenstein, "Egocentric Empathy Gaps Between Owners and Buyers: Misperceptions of the Endowment Effect," *Journal of Personality and Social Psychology* 79 (2000): 66–76.
5. Antoine Bechara, Hannah Damasio, Daniel Tranel, and Antonio R. Damasio, "Deciding Advantageously Before Knowing the Advantageous Strategy," *Science* 275 (1997): 1293–1295.
6. J. Frank Yates, *Judgment and Decision Making* (Upper Saddle River, NJ: Prentice Hall, 1990). (See Chapters 8–11, especially.)
7. W. V. Harlow and Keith C. Brown, "Understanding and Assessing Financial Risk Tolerance: A Biological Perspective," *Financial Analysts Journal* 46 (November-December 1990): 50–62.
8. Ralph O. Swalm, "Utility Theory—Insights into Risk Taking," *Harvard Business Review* 48 (November-December 1966): 113–126.
9. Robert C. Higgins, *Analysis for Financial Management* (5th ed.) (Boston: Irwin McGraw-Hill, 1998).

Chapter Eight

1. Winston R. Sieck and J. Frank Yates, "Exposition Effects on Decision Making: Choice and Confidence in Choice," *Organizational Behavior and Human Decision Processes,* 70 (1997): 207–219.

2. Barry M. Staw, Sigal G. Barsade, and Kenneth W. Koput, "Escalation at the Credit Window: A Longitudinal Study of Bank Executives' Recognition and Write-Off of Problem Loans," *Journal of Applied Psychology* 82 (1997): 130–142.

3. Danny Ertel, "Turning Negotiation into a Corporate Capability," *Harvard Business Review* 77, no. 3 (1999): 55ff.

4. Steven Thomma, "Battered Women Denied Insurance," *Detroit Free Press* (May 13, 1994): 1A.

5. Edwin O. Reischauer and Marius B. Jansen, *The Japanese Today* (Cambridge, MA: Belknap, 1995).

6. Roger Buehler, Dale Griffin, and Lee Ross, "Exploring the 'Planning Fallacy': Why People Underestimate Their Task Completion Times," *Journal of Personality* & *Social Psychology* 67 (1994): 366–381.

The Author

J. Frank Yates is a professor of business administration and marketing as well as a professor of psychology at the University of Michigan. He was also the university's first Arthur F. Thurnau Professor of Psychology. In addition, he serves as the coordinator of the University of Michigan's Decision Consortium, which is a university-wide distributed center for decision scholarship. Yates received his bachelor's degree from the University of Notre Dame (maxima cum laude). He earned his master's and Ph.D. degrees at the University of Michigan, where he was a National Science Foundation Fellow and a Woodrow Wilson Fellow. He has been a visiting professor at Rice University in Houston, Leiden University in the Netherlands, Peking University in China, and the University of Tokyo in Japan. A fellow of the American Psychological Association and the American Psychological Society, Yates has received several awards, including an American Psychological Association Teaching Award and a Best Competitive Paper Award from the Association for Consumer Research.

Frank Yates's work seeks to achieve a deep understanding of how people decide naturally and to help them decide better, in virtually every context, and especially in businesses and other organizations. Thus, over the years, he and his collaborators have studied decision processes and developed tools for decision making in an array of domains from employee testing to financial forecasting, medical diagnosis and treatment, consumer choice, judgment accuracy analysis, risk perception, accountability, ambiguity, and cross-cultural variations in decision customs. His work has been published in dozens of scientific papers as well as books, including his own *Judgment and Decision Making* (Prentice Hall) and *Risk-Taking Behavior* (Wiley).

Frank Yates is a past president of the Society for Judgment and Decision Making. He spent several years as a member of the National Research Council's Committee on Human Factors as well as the National Science Foundation's Decision, Risk, and Management Science Review Panel. He is the founding and current associate editor of the *Journal of Behavioral Decision Making* and a longtime member of the editorial board of *Organizational Behavior and Human Decision Processes*. He has been on the editorial boards of numerous other journals, too, including *Medical Decision Making* and the *Journal of Applied Psychology*.

Decision problems and phenomena of all kinds, and particularly those concerning any aspect of how companies decide and might decide better, hold a special fascination for Frank Yates. He can be reached at jfyates@umich.edu.

Index

A

Academy of Management Executives, 202

Accept/reject decisions: defined, 27; 3+ Rule applied to, 55–56

Acceptability (cardinal decision issue 9), 175–189; authority convention changes and, 71; to co-beneficiaries, 185–187; to co-deciders, 179–185; collective decision making and, 67–68, 188; of compensatory *versus* non-compensatory tradeoff methods, 166–167; description of, 13, 15, 175–177; disasters of, 177–179; hazards and challenges of, listed, 193; implementation problems and, 189–190; issue, stated, 177; of nonhuman consultants, 134; nonpetitioners and, 188–189; petitioners and, 187–188; preventing disasters of, 177–179; process objections and, 181–182; to pure stakeholders, 187–189; recommendations for, listed, 193; self-interest objections and, 182–184; stakeholders/objectors and, 179–189; summary of, 192–193; values and, 143; wisdom objections and, 180–182

Acceptability checklist, 178–179, 186, 188–189

Accuracy suppressors, 135–138

Action plan, decision management, 198–204; institution element of, 199–204, 205; partnership element of, 198–199

Affective part of brain, 146–147

Affordability concerns, obliviousness and, 53

Agents, decision, 82–83; Behavior Prediction Law for, 84–85; consultants *versus*, 83, 102; costs of, 84; delegation cost principle and, 89; incentive misalignment of, 85; mode of using, 82–83, 84; nonhuman, 83; selection of, 84–85; self-interest objections and, 182–183

Aggregated outcomes, as criterion for effective decisions, 34–35. *See also* Outcomes